BIBLICAL TIMES

Palace officials, carved in relief, display the dignity of the mighty
Persian Empire (at its peak c.550-480 B.C.).

Pharaoh Ramses II filled Egypt with temples and huge statues – further glorifying himself by the simple means of adding his own name to earlier works.

HISTORICAL FACTS
BIBLICAL TIMES

AMANDA O'NEILL

A breakthrough in the military technology of the ancient world, the war chariot helped to create empires. This bronze model is from the Assyrian Empire (1530-612 B.C.)

CRESCENT BOOKS
NEW YORK • AVENEL, NEW JERSEY

CLB 2837

© 1992 Colour Library Books Ltd., Godalming, Surrey, England.

This 1992 edition published by Crescent Books,
distributed by Outlet Book Company, Inc.,
a Random House Company
40 Engelhard Avenue, Avenel, New Jersey 07001

Printed and bound in Italy

ISBN 0 517 06560 6

8 7 6 5 4 3 2 1

The Author
Amanda O'Neill was born in Sussex, England, in 1951, and studied Anglo-Saxon, Old Norse, and Middle English literature at the University of Exeter. Her specialist field of interest lies in the Celtic myths and medieval romances of King Arthur. She has edited and written books on topics ranging from the decorative arts to natural history, and is currently engaged in a study of the history of domesticated animals and their association with humans.

Credits
Editor: Richard O'Neill
Designer: Jill Coote
Map artwork: Peter Bull
Picture Editor: Miriam Sharland
Production: Ruth Arthur, Sally Connolly, Andrew Whitelaw
Director of Production: Gerald Hughes
Typesetting: SX Composing Ltd.
Color separations: Scantrans Pte Ltd., Singapore
Printed and bound by New Interlitho SpA, Italy

Philistine coffins of the 14th-13th century B.C. are modeled in stylized human form, with folded hands and wide, staring eyes.

CONTENTS

Introduction

The Bible is the world's all time best selling book. Its name comes from the Latinized Greek words *Ta Biblia*, meaning 'The Books,' but Christians also know it as the 'Holy Scriptures,' the 'Word of God,' or simply the 'Good Book.' It is sacred to all Christian believers, some of whom regard every one of its words as literal truth. Others, no less sincere in their beliefs, prefer to interpret parts of it, especially the earlier books of the Old Testament, in the light of modern scientific thought.

The Bible had its origin as a record of the history, from the creation of the world onward, and the development of the religious laws of a numerically small and apparently unimportant people. These were the Hebrews (later called Israelites, or Jews), who lived in a tiny country whose chief significance was that it lay between the great ancient civilizations of Mesopotamia and Egypt. To the ancient books now known as the Old Testament was added, in the 1st and 2nd centuries A.D., the New Testament. This too was the record of what many would then have considered an obscure people. It recorded the life and teachings of the founder of what was then a minority religious sect, Christianity. The writers of the Old and New Testaments perhaps never realized that their works, collected in the Bible, would become the most widely read – and probably the most influential – book in human history.

Today the 24 books of the Old Testament that form the Hebrew Bible – of which the first five, the *Pentateuch* (Greek: 'five books'), constitute the *Torah* ('the Law') – are the most sacred writings of the Jewish religion. The Bible as a whole, combining Old and New Testaments, is the holiest book of the Christian religion. However, different Christian demoninations vary in the number of books of the Old Testament their versions of the Bible include. For example, the King James (Authorized Version) used by many Protestants includes 39 books of the Old Testament. Roman Catholic Bibles add seven more books (sometimes also printed in Protestant Bibles as the *Apocrypha*; the word means 'hidden away,' and indicates that their authority is not fully recognized), to which the Greek Orthodox Church adds five more. The New Testament's 27 books are accepted by all Christians.

The *Torah*, the sacred writings of Judaism, is written in Hebrew on parchment scrolls, with covers of velvet, silk or brocade. These scrolls are of the 16th-18th century.

The so-called Tomb of Zechariah, Jerusalem, is actually the Greek-influenced mausoleum of a priestly house of c.200 B.C.

This book is not an examination of the Bible, but an attempt to provide a brief account of the world as it was in the times that the Bible came into being. The books of the Bible span nearly 2,000 years of the history of lands and peoples far distanced from us by both time and customs. But our Western culture owes to those far off peoples not only two major religions, but also many aspects of its laws, social attitudes, and language. When we speak of 'Biblical Times' or 'Bible Lands,' we think of Palestine: 'Promised Land' of the Jews; the 'Holy Land' of Christian pilgrims. But Palestine did not exist in isolation. The key to its historical importance lay in its relationships with neighboring countries and cultures.

In early Old Testament times, the Jews (Hebrews, as they were then called) were landless nomads whose wanderings brought them into contact with the civilizations of Mesopotamia and Egypt. This interchange of cultures did not end when they settled in Israel. For that was a land corridor through which passed the great trade-routes of Africa, Asia, and Europe, exposing the land of the Jews to the impact of many peoples. Often the impact of other cultures was made by force. The empires of the Middle East – Egypt, Assyria, Babylonia, Greece, and Rome – vied for possession of this strategically sited country. Only twice in Old Testament times, under King David (*pages 46-47*) and under the Hasmonean Dynasty (*pages 58-59*) was Israel an independent kingdom. The New Testament brings us into the realms of the Roman Empire. This history of Bible lands and peoples is, therefore, not confined to Palestine, but extends from ancient civilizations which had an impact on the earliest Jewish people to the lands of early Christendom.

The Bible story begins in Mesopotamia, 'Land of Two Rivers,' said to be tributaries of the river which Genesis tells us ran out of Eden. The Tigris and Euphrates Rivers water a fertile area which forms one horn of the 'Fertile Crescent' of the Middle East – a crescent-shaped expanse of well-watered land between the desert and the sea. Most scholars believe it was in the Tigris-Euphrates valley, in c.8000 B.C., that farming was invented. Cultivated fields meant a settled lifestyle and led to further innovations.

The ancient world keeps many secrets. Is the intense gaze of this figure (a Sumerian temple statue, c.2600 B.C.) that of a worshiper or the god himself?

Before 4000 B.C., the valley farmers controlled the rivers: banks and ditches held back floods; canals watered outlying fields. Large scale irrigation meant that more productive fields supported a larger population. This in turn demanded more complex social organization, with a class structure of leaders, managers, and laborers. Surplus food production was traded, producing wealth that allowed the development of a standard of living far beyond subsistence level. Tools were developed to maintain this standard: math, calendars, money, weights and measures, record-keeping by the new invention of writing. The Tigris-Euphrates valley was the home of the earliest known civilization, that of the Sumerians (*pages 24-25*), soon followed by similar developments in Egypt's Nile Valley, creating the kingdoms of ancient Egypt (*pages 28-35*).

Mesopotamia has been called 'the cradle of civilization,' not only because of its agricultural revolution and Sumerian Empire, but also because, over the centuries, trade and invasion made it a cultural melting pot, from which new ideas and techniques were spread. This created the world of the early Old Testament, where the nomadic

Hebrews came into contact with Babylonians, Elamites, Hittites, Phoenicians, Assyrians, Persians, and Egyptians.

Only in fairly recent times have we gained knowledge of some of these ancient civilizations. Until about the 18th century, 'ancient history' began with Greece and Rome. Then archeologists began to uncover 'legendary' cities like Babylon, Nineveh, and Nimrud. Scholars were astounded by the revelation of great empires existing 3,000 years before the dawn of the classical world. Sir Austen Henry Layard (1817-1894), who excavated the mound of Nineveh, recorded his awe at finding among 'the wretchedness and ignorance of a few half-barbarous tribes . . . ruins and shapeless heaps of earth,' evidence of 'the luxury and civilization of a mighty nation.'

The kingdoms of Ancient Egypt did not completely disappear from human memory, because their greatest monuments, the pyramids, survived for all to see. Yet little was known about them. Early in the 19th century the French leader Napoleon Bonaparte invaded Egypt. He got little military benefit – but had a tremendous effect on archaeological development. His politically inspired interest in the monuments of the Pharaohs sparked off a train of investigation which still continues. Tombs, temples, and statues buried for centuries came to light, revealing a magnificent civilization. Grave goods ranged from splendors like the famous treasure of Tutankhamun, revealed in

The glory of a mighty nation: one of the reliefs that adorned the palace of Persepolis, heart of the Persian Empire.

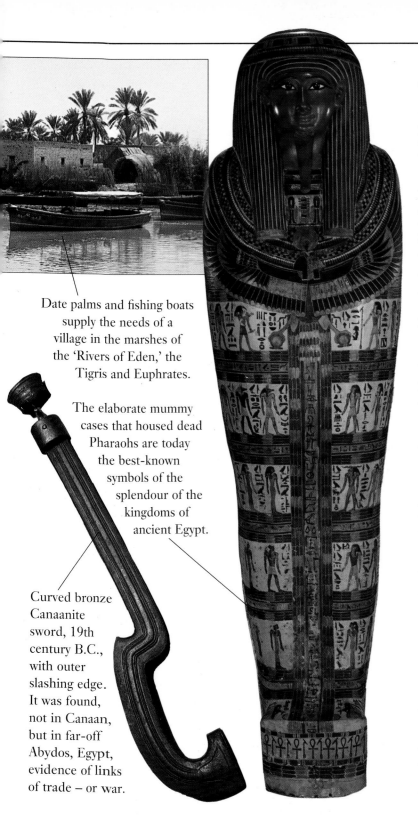

Date palms and fishing boats supply the needs of a village in the marshes of the 'Rivers of Eden,' the Tigris and Euphrates.

The elaborate mummy cases that housed dead Pharaohs are today the best-known symbols of the splendour of the kingdoms of ancient Egypt.

Curved bronze Canaanite sword, 19th century B.C., with outer slashing edge. It was found, not in Canaan, but in far-off Abydos, Egypt, evidence of links of trade – or war.

empires run through the Old Testament. But while the mighty civilizations of the Middle East rose and fell, the Hebrews' achievement endures. They were never a powerful people. They were enslaved by Egypt and Babylon; fought to retain their little land against Canaanites and Philistines; strove to maintain their own law and religion against the power of Greece and Rome. They left no impressive physical monuments. For generations they were tent-dwellers who made little mark on the land; and when at last they began to raise buildings like Solomon's Temple (*pages 48-49*), these were destroyed by more powerful foes. The factor which enabled them to endure when greater cultures fell, and their lasting monument, was their religion. They were the first people to devote themselves to a single God, an unseen, all powerful divinity. Their religious beliefs were to influence the history of lands far beyond their own.

Ancient Jewish tradition, preserved in the Hebrew Bible and other great books of Judaic law, holds that it was Abraham, founder of the Hebrew nation (somewhere around 2000-1700 B.C.), who first rejected the idols of his ancestors and to whom the One God was revealed. In early Old Testament times Abraham's descendants sometimes veered from this belief to worship the gods of the peoples among whom they lived. Some scholars think that the early Hebrews had not yet fully evolved the concept of the one, true God, but worshipped their own principal divinity while still paying homage to lesser gods. During the years of the Exodus (*pages 34-35*), when they journeyed through the wilderness to their Promised Land, their leader Moses fought against the worship of idols to unite his people in belief in the One God. The task was not completed in his lifetime, but by the 5th century B.C., following the preaching of prophets like Ezra and the devoted work of scribes who worked to mold the books of the Torah into a single authority, the worship of the One God was truly achieved.

1917, to wall-paintings illustrating daily life. Above all there were written inscriptions – hieroglyphs which scholars studied doggedly for years until they yielded up their secrets, making it possible to read eyewitness accounts of ancient Egypt.

The Hebrews' encounters with these great

Under the rule of the Roman Empire, with the kingdom of Israel shrunk to the little province of Judaea, Judaism gave birth to a new religion. Jesus Christ, recognized by the Jewish faith as a great teacher, was to his followers something more: Messiah ('the Anointed One'), the Son of God, born as a man to save the world. His teachings were based on Judaic principles, and despite opposition from orthodox Jews and pagans alike, quickly spread. After His Crucifixion, His followers carried His teachings far across the known world.

Within half a century of Jesus's time on Earth, Christianity was firmly enough established to survive savage persecution. Part of its appeal lay in its message of hope to the world's underdogs – the poor, the outcasts, the slaves – who were told that in God's sight they were equal with their masters, and even had advantages their betters lacked. Jesus specifically blessed the poor, promising that those who had nothing in this world still had the love of God, and that by following Him they could win eternal happiness in a kingdom 'not of this world.'

Another vital factor in the spread of Christianity was that it answered a need not fully met by other religions: it made sense of human existence. When St. Paulinus preached the Gospel in the British kingdom of Northumbria in 627, the pagan high priest himself was among the first to declare that the new religion was an improvement on his own. One of the king's men supported him, comparing life to the flight of a sparrow through a lighted room, passing from a dark winter night into brightness, then back into darkness. 'Of what went before, or what is to follow,' he commented, 'we are utterly ignorant. If, therefore, this new doctrine contains something more certain, it seems justly to deserve to be followed.' Northumbria was swiftly converted, like many communities before and after.

Christianity has come a long way since the time of Jesus – and some say it has taken wrong turnings. Jesus Himself was unconventionally tolerant for His time. The 'friend of tax-collectors and sinners,' He welcomed those seen as socially undesirable. When strict Jews closed their ranks against outsiders, He befriended the despised Samaritans and welcomed the faith of Gentiles (non-Jews). In a society which saw women as possessions, He accepted them as valued followers.

Early Christians, hiding in Rome's catacombs, painted Jesus as the Good Shepherd on the walls for their comfort.

A 5th century ivory carving shows St. Peter, like Moses, striking water from rock – but Peter's Rock is the Church.

But His teachings have often been interpreted in ways that surely would have displeased Him.

His Apostles and their successors had elaborated on His message, and from around the 2nd century the scholars now known as the 'Fathers of the Church' applied the principles of classical philosophy to Christ's teachings. This led to arguments, sometimes violent, between Christians who accepted different interpretations of the faith. Many sincere believers who differed, even on quite minor matters, from the ruling authorities of the Church were denounced as 'heretics,' and expelled. The early Church Fathers created an anti-feminist movement, built on the writings of St. Paul rather than the words of Jesus. They blamed the Fall of Man on Eve; described woman as 'the Devil's gateway;' and established a Church in which 'Man commands, woman obeys.'

The growth of the Church's social and political power after its recognition by Emperor Constantine (*pages 84-85*) produced much corruption among the clergy, from ruthless popes to the notoriously worldly friars of the Middle Ages, of whom a song of c.1380 says: 'There shall no soul have room in

The later Church saw woman as man's inferior, yet at the same time increasingly revered Mary, Mother of Jesus (depicted here in stained glass at Chartres Cathedral, France).

Hell, Of friars there is such throng' (i.e., 'There are so many friars in Hell that there isn't room for anyone else'). By that time many Christians favored the conversion of heathens by force, like the medieval King Olaf (St. Olaf) of Norway, who offered his subjects the choice between baptism or 'loss of life, and limbs, and property.' Christians often viewed non-Christians as lower forms of life, whom it was virtuous to abuse: this led to centuries of persecution of the Jews, and to the savagery of the Crusades against the Muslims.

All too often, down the centuries, Christians have forgotten the words of Jesus as reported in the Gospel of St. John (Chapter 13; Verse 34): 'A new commandment I give unto you, That ye love one another; as I have loved you, that ye also love one another.'

In the beginning

Scientists believe that the entire solar system originated in a formless mass of gas (a solar nebula), which by some 5 billion years ago built up into our Sun and planets. Earth – blazing hot and surrounded by deadly gases – could not support life until its surface cooled down and its poisonous atmosphere evolved into breathable air. This took millions of years. Water covered much of the planet's surface, and in these oceans, perhaps c.3.5 million years ago, life first appeared. The seas formed a 'primal soup' of the basic elements that make up living organisms, and some of these molecules fused together to form very simple life forms. Later still, some of these – the first plants – developed green chlorophyll pigments, allowing them to use energy from sunlight to process their own food from water and carbon dioxide. This paved the way for the next stage: the development of animal life. The Book of Genesis describes God's creation of 'the heaven and the earth' as an act in six stages: the Six Days of Creation. Earth is created first, with plant life on the third day, the first animal life in the waters on the fifth day, and land animals

'And God said, Let us make man in our image' (Genesis I 26) – in Judaic-Christian tradition the climax of the Six Days of Creation. Renaissance artist Michelangelo depicts the first man, Adam, as God's perfect creation.

and man himself on the sixth day. The Bible story may be seen as a symbolic parallel to the scientific account, although some Christians, called 'fundamentalists,' accept only the biblical version. Most ancient peoples believed that life began in the waters. The oldest known Creation story, that of the Sumerians, makes the ocean, Nammu, the beginning of all things and mother of Heaven and Earth. Later stages of creation come from Enki (fresh water) and Nintu (the fertile earth).

Rival creator gods like the Canaanites' Baal (center, between Sun and Moon gods) were eventually to be ousted by the Jewish God.

A star is born. A spectacular sight granted to us by modern telescopes, the nebula is invisible to the naked eye. Scientists today believe our planet began in just such glorious chaos, taking millions of years to become habitable.

❏ Many scientists believe the Sun and planets were created by a great explosion in space – the 'Big Bang' – which scattered gas and dust to form galaxies. But the 'Steady State' theory holds that the galaxies were formed at different times, with hydrogen gas produced in space continuously creating new masses of matter.

❏ In the Babylonian Epic of Creation (c.1000 B.C.), Tiamat, the ocean, is Mother of all Creation – but her children's noise angers her and she turns to destroy them. When she is slain by the god Marduk, her body forms heaven and earth; then Marduk creates man to serve the gods.

❏ In the 19th century, the study of fossils led scientists like Charles Darwin (below) to propose that all life – including man – had developed from earlier, more primitive forms. Today, many people accept Darwin's theory of evolution, but others believe that Genesis is literally true, and that all creatures were first made in their modern form.

The gardens of Eden

Scholars have long debated the geographical location of the Garden of Eden, where the Bible sets the creation of humankind. Genesis gives its position in relation to named rivers and countries, but research has not established a site more definite than 'somewhere in Mesopotamia,' usually in the plains between the Tigris and Euphrates Rivers. A number of other sites have been suggested, in modern Iraq, India, and Ethiopia.

Medieval scholars believed that Eden lay just beyond the limits of the known world, awaiting discovery and still in a state of perfection, unlike the rest of the world which had been contaminated by human sin. Later, when 19th century scholars trying to make sense of fossil remains suggested that life began in a land now lost under the sea, some people seized on the idea that this 'lost continent' was the true Eden. Many modern thinkers take Eden to be an imaginary picture of perfection, not an actual place. They sometimes attach the name to archeological sites associated with the earliest fossil human remains, like Olduvai Gorge in Kenya. Popular sentiment holds that 'we are nearer to God in a garden than anywhere else on earth,' and from Eden onward the garden has been a favorite image of religious writers. The Song of Solomon gave medieval writers and artists the theme of the *hortus conclusus* ('enclosed garden'), a quiet place where a godly person cultivates his or her soul. The garden is also a frequent symbol in non-Christian belief: the Greeks' Garden of the Hesperides, where the golden apples of youth grew; the enchanted gardens of the pagan Celtic Otherworld; and the gardens of the Muslim paradise.

The serpent (later identified with Satan) tempts Adam and Eve to eat the forbidden fruit – the crime of disobedience which will cause their exile from Eden.

The Bible's tale of Adam's progression, from finding plentiful food in Eden, to tilling the ground after his exile, parallels the scientific view of early men's development from food-gatherers to farmers.

❏ The Alexandrian Jews who first put the Hebrew scriptures (Old Testament) into Greek in the 3rd century B.C. translated Eden as 'Paradise.' This Greek word was borrowed from Persian, where it referred to the beautiful pleasure gardens created for Persian kings. Early Christian writers used it to refer to Heaven, as we still do.

❏ Some 19th-century scientists believed life began in prehistoric 'lost continents,' long sunk beneath the sea. Lemuria, a vast land bridge linking Africa and Malaysia, was invented by a zoologist to solve the puzzle of similar life forms found in lands separated by the sea. Mu, in the Pacific Ocean, was invented by scholars misreading the Mayan alphabet of Central America. Geologists have found no evidence for the existence of either, but it was once thought that Lemuria or Mu was the original Garden of Eden where humanity first appeared.

Flemish painter Jan Brueghel (1568-1625) portrayed the Garden of Eden as the 'Earthly Paradise,' the earth in a state of perfection.

Tradition says all beasts were created vegetarian in Eden, living together peaceably with neither hunters nor hunted.

To anthropologists, the true 'Eden,' the birth-place of mankind, is Olduvai Gorge, Tanzania, site of the earliest human remains yet discovered.

The world outside Eden

The Bible tells how humanity's history began with the expulsion of Adam and Eve from Eden into the world outside, which they peopled with their descendants. Fundamentalist Christians believe that every word of Genesis is literal truth: they say humankind began with Adam and Eve, physically perfect specimens of men and women like ourselves. But most scientists today believe that humans evolved gradually from ape-like ancestors – part of a long process of evolution from the very first single-celled life forms. But whether we believe that Adam's son Abel, or a tribe of Stone Age men, first cultivated land, it was the development of farming that brought the dawn of civilization. It created the first settled communities, leading in time to cities and the growth of urban culture. Most scholars think farming began in the Middle East in c.8000 B.C., in the well-watered plains of the Tigris, Euphrates, and Nile Rivers. This area, called the 'Fertile Crescent,' is usually considered the cradle of civilization. The landscape of modern Israel is marked by many huge mounds, or tels, formed by the accumulated debris of ancient cities. The 50ft (15m) high mound of Tel es-Sultan at Jericho records the history of one of the world's oldest continuously inhabited towns. Now best known for its conquest by the Israelites in c.1230 B.C. (*pages 36-37*), Jericho was occupied from c.9000 B.C. onward; by c.7000 it was a walled settlement housing some 2,000 Stone Age farmers. As trade routes were established across the desert, Jericho, an oasis with a freshwater spring, became an important junction, and by the time of the patriarch Abraham it was a major city.

A face from Stone Age Jericho. The walled city of c.7000 B.C. yielded skulls with plaster features and shell eyes: perhaps honored ancestors.

The household trash and building rubble of Israel's ancient cities outlasted the cities themselves as mounds, or tels – urban monuments whose layers tell a story of repeated resettlements.

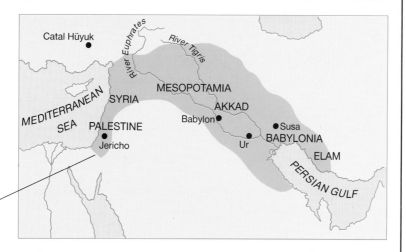

The great tel of Jericho bears witness to the scale of the late Stone Age city, with stone walls and massive round tower.

In the Fertile Crescent, watered by three great rivers, farmers could grow enough food to support large populations. This made possible the growth of cities – and civilization.

Map labels: Catal Hüyuk, River Euphrates, River Tigris, MEDITERRANEAN SEA, SYRIA, MESOPOTAMIA, PALESTINE, AKKAD, Babylon, Jericho, Ur, Susa, BABYLONIA, ELAM, PERSIAN GULF

❑ The Bible tells us that God was so angered by Adam and Eve's disobedience that he not only condemned them to hard labor farming ('In the sweat of thy face shalt thou eat bread . . .') outside Eden, but also decreed the earth they tilled should be infested with 'thorns . . . and thistles.'

❑ The Bible's story of the murder of the farmer Abel by his brother Cain, a hunter, reflects the long struggle between settled and nomadic peoples. This extended from earliest times into the 19th and 20th centuries: to the 'range wars' of the American West; to the persecution of gypsies, peddlers, and other 'traveling people' (like the Kurds of Iraq and Turkey) today.

❑ Catal Hüyük (Turkey) (below), another of the world's oldest towns, was settled in c. 7000 B.C. and soon became a trade center extending over c.32 acres (13ha). Its people lived in small, mud brick houses, built so close together that access was apparently via the roof. Shrines decorated with paintings and relief modelings show that its people worshiped the bull – king of the herds of cattle on which their economy depended.

The great flood

The rivers that gave fertility to Mesopotamia's plains could also destroy, with floods. It is not surprising that Hebrew tradition remembered the land's devastation by water. Genesis tells how God, angered by men's wickedness, sent the Flood to destroy them – all but the virtuous Noah, who was told to build a huge boat, the Ark, to preserve his family along with breeding pairs of every animal. When the Flood abated, the Ark's occupants were the only survivors. Historically, ancient Mesopotamia saw several major floods. The worst, which overwhelmed the city of Ur in c.4000 B.C., burying it under some 10ft (3m) of silt, is sometimes identified with the Flood of Genesis, although some scholars prefer to believe in a literally universal deluge. The peoples of ancient Mesopotamia – Sumerians and Babylonians – recorded a flood myth in the story of Gilgamesh, an epic with roots in the third millennium B.C. It tells how the gods resolved to destroy mankind with a flood, but one man, warned by the creator god Ea, built a boat to save himself and 'the seed of all living things.' The story has many details in common with that told in Genesis, and is clearly related, although scholars have not resolved which account is the older. The significant difference lies in the Hebrews' concept, unique in their time, of a single God with a close personal relationship with His people. It is only in the Hebrew account that God establishes a covenant with Noah and his family, promising never again to destroy His creation.

In this charming 15th century picture of Noah's Ark, the animals crammed in 'two by two' seem to leave little room for food, baggage, or even Noah and his family.

Best known for building the Ark, Noah was also a farmer, credited with introducing vineyards – and founding a wine-making industry.

The peoples of Sumer and Babylon recorded their own flood myth. It survives as part of the epic of the hero Gilgamesh, seen here battling with lions.

The Ark is said to have landed on Mount Ararat, Turkey – so 19th century Bible scholars took fossil shells found here to be screws from the Ark.

After the Flood, the rainbow: token of God's vow that 'the water shall no more become a flood to destroy all flesh.'

FACT FILE

❑ Based on the biblical account, the measurements of Noah's Ark have been reckoned at c.450ft (137m) length, 75ft (23m) beam, and 46ft (14m) draft – about half the size of a modern Atlantic liner like the 53,000 ton *United States*. One zoologist calculated that the Ark must have carried 2,500,000 animals; a lower estimate (excluding creatures which could have survived outside the Ark) is 35,000.

❑ In the oldest Sumerian texts the 'Noah' figure is called Ziusudra; in the Assyrian cycle he is Utnapishtim; and in Babylonian texts he is Atramhasis. A Hittite version calls him Na-ah-mu-u-li-el, a name apparently related to that of Noah.

❑ In both Mesopotamian and Hebrew tradition, the Flood is caused by divine wrath at human evil. Noah takes his family and pairs of every animal on his Ark; Utnapishtim takes 'my family . . . the beasts of the field . . . and all the craftsmen.' Both boats settle on mountains – Mount Ararat and Mount Nisir. When the waters recede, Noah releases first a raven, then a dove to seek dry land: Utnapishtim sends a dove, then a swallow, and last a raven. Both sacrifice when the waters subside.

❑ Flood myths occur elsewhere. India's 'Noah' is Manu, saved with his wife from the waters by the god Vishnu.

Sumer: land of Abraham

In southeast Mesopotamia, the Sumerians developed one of the world's oldest civilizations. Originally wandering hunters, they settled in Sumer c.5000-4000 B.C. They created extensive drainage and irrigation systems to transform the Tigris-Euphrates floodplains into productive fields, and established a farming culture. Under the rule of their priesthood, a highly organized society evolved. By c.3500 its trade and religious centers had grown into powerful city-states, including Eridu, Uruk, Lagash, Umma, Kish, and Ur. Their organizational demands led the priest-administrators to develop a new tool, writing: at first a picture script, but by c.3200 a phonetic alphabet, called cuneiform ('wedge-shaped' – from the letter shapes). Many thousand inscribed clay tablets survive, from temple accounts to personal letters. Another innovation was the wheel, revolutionizing both transport and (in the form of the potter's wheel) the production of domestic goods. As their wealth increased, the Sumerian cities were troubled both by raiding tribes and inter-city rivalry. They appointed war leaders, who by c.3000 took power from the priesthood and became hereditary kings. Under kingly rule, Ur became Mesopotamia's richest city. Its royal cemetery (c.2500) has yielded some of the finest treasures of Sumerian craftsmanship. A few centuries later, Sumer was conquered; but Ur was to achieve lasting fame as the birthplace, perhaps some time before 2000 B.C., of the Biblical patriarch Abraham.

Sumerian goldsmiths created fine work like this bull's head ornament adorning a superb lyre from Ur, 2600-2400 B.C.

The proud bull's head is gold on a wooden core, the inlaid decoration mother-of-pearl and lapis lazuli. The Royal Cemetery of Ur yielded several harps and lyres decorated in this style.

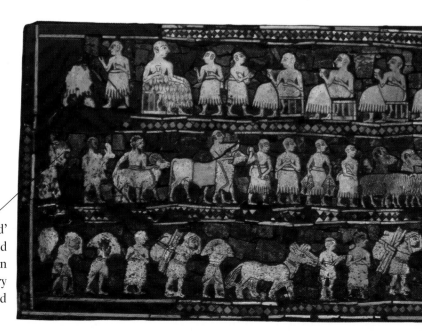

The 'Royal Standard' of Ur is a double-sided mosaic plaque of unknown purpose, perhaps a military standard – or the sounding board of a musical instrument.

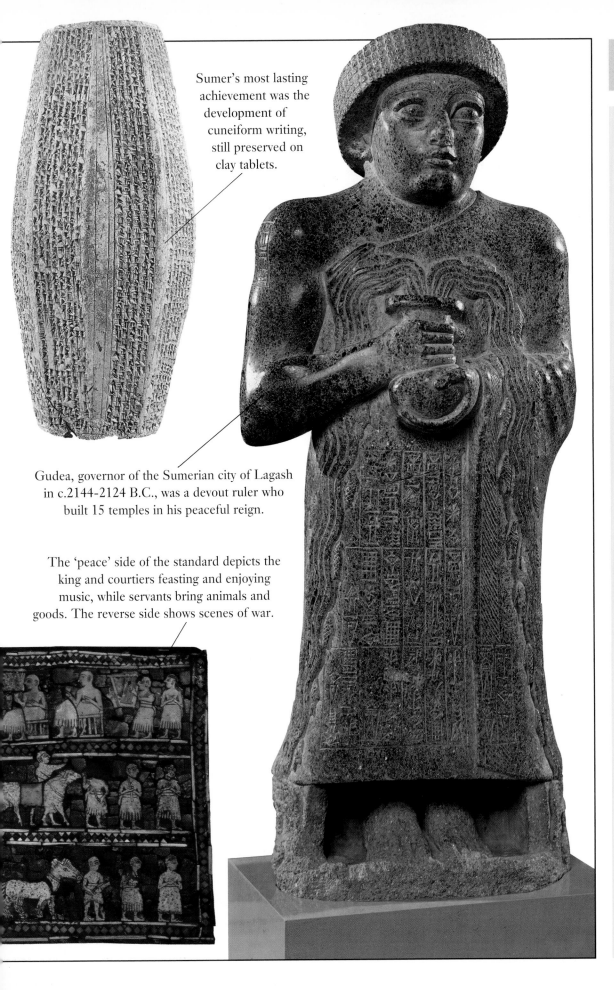

Sumer's most lasting achievement was the development of cuneiform writing, still preserved on clay tablets.

Gudea, governor of the Sumerian city of Lagash in c.2144-2124 B.C., was a devout ruler who built 15 temples in his peaceful reign.

The 'peace' side of the standard depicts the king and courtiers feasting and enjoying music, while servants bring animals and goods. The reverse side shows scenes of war.

❑ Lacking a supply of building stone or timber, Sumerian architects used sun-dried mud bricks to erect temples on high platforms. The White Temple at Uruk (its bricks dramatically whitewashed) stood on a platform 230ft (70m) long and 43ft (13m) high. Such raised temples eventually led to the ziggurats – stepped platforms – of Assyrian and Babylonian architecture.

❑ A Sumerian legal document of c.2350 B.C. records that penalties for crimes were to include a written statement of the offence. Thus the guilt of a convicted adulteress was written on the stones used to stone her to death; while a woman who said to a man 'something she should not have said' had her crime recorded on bricks, which were used to crush her teeth.

❑ A Sumerian king of c.2500 B.C. achieved unique and enduring fame when he became the hero of a cycle of mythical poems. The *Epic of Gilgamesh* survives in Assyrian versions from c.1800 and c.1200 B.C., and is thought to pre-date Homer's *Iliad* by some 1500 years. Little is known of the historical King Gilgamesh of Uruk, although he is said to have built Uruk's great city walls and restored a lost sanctuary at Nippur.

❑ Ur housed the world's first museum – the collection of the princess Ennigaldi-Nanna, kept in one of the temples.

Babel and Old Babylon

Sumer's city-states never formed a united empire. This was left to their northern neighbors, a Semitic-speaking people called the Akkadians (from their capital, Akkad). In c.2300 B.C., their leader Sargon the Great conquered Sumer and most of Mesopotamia, to found the world's first great empire. Sumerian culture was absorbed into Akkadian; the Akkadian language (an early form of Babylonian) largely replaced that of Sumer. Sargon's descendants ruled for about 100 years. A later ruler, Ur-Nammu, took the title of King of Sumer and Akkad and founded a new, powerful dynasty at Ur. His successors were unable to hold the kingdom: in 2006, Ur fell to the Elamites – Sumer's traditional enemies.

Sargon the Great's palace at his new capital of Khorsabad (ancient Dur-Sharrukin, 'city of Sargon') was adorned with huge statues and reliefs. This one depicts the hero Gilgamesh.

From the ensuing tribal warfare, the Amorites (another Semitic group) emerged triumphant in c.1990, to found the Old Babylonian Empire. Their greatest ruler, Hammurabi (c.1792-1750), extended Babylonian rule by both conquest and peaceful trade. He introduced fair and comprehensive legislation (which often resembles the laws of Moses recorded in Exodus). Under Hammurabi, the city of Babylon became the empire's capital. The Tower of Babel – where humankind was punished for its blasphemous ambition in trying to build a tower that would reach heaven by being made to speak different languages – is sometimes identified with Babylon's great temple-tower of the god Marduk. While the Amorites settled in Sumer's cities, at least one group turned back to the older nomadic way of life: Abraham led his family from the city of Ur, his birthplace, to seek the land promised to him by God, and to found a great nation.

Legend says Sargon of Akkad was the adopted son of a poor farmer. He rose to become cupbearer to the king of Kish (north Sumer), then master of Mesopotamia.

Gilgamesh, commonly shown (as here) wrestling a lion, is hero of the world's oldest epic. The Babylonians adopted his story from their Sumerian predecessors.

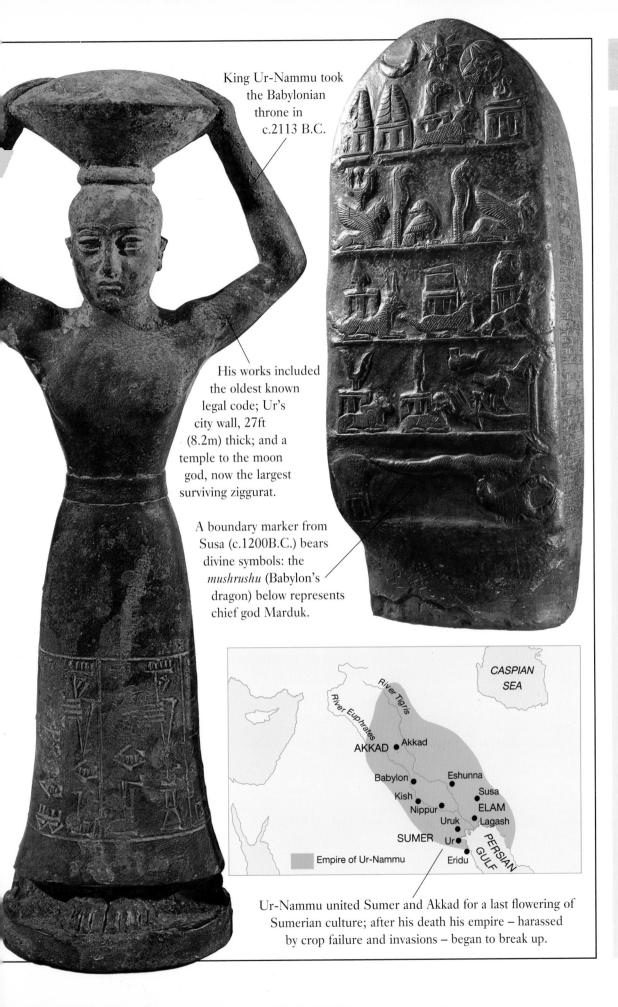

King Ur-Nammu took the Babylonian throne in c.2113 B.C.

His works included the oldest known legal code; Ur's city wall, 27ft (8.2m) thick; and a temple to the moon god, now the largest surviving ziggurat.

A boundary marker from Susa (c.1200B.C.) bears divine symbols: the *mushrushu* (Babylon's dragon) below represents chief god Marduk.

Ur-Nammu united Sumer and Akkad for a last flowering of Sumerian culture; after his death his empire – harassed by crop failure and invasions – began to break up.

CASPIAN SEA

River Tigris
River Euphrates
AKKAD • Akkad
Babylon • Eshunna
Kish • Susa
Nippur • ELAM
Uruk • Lagash
SUMER Ur •
Eridu • PERSIAN GULF

Empire of Ur-Nammu

FACT FILE

❏ The Semitic tribes – said to be descendants of Noah's son Shem – spoke a language related to both modern Arabic and Hebrew.

❏ The Amorites introduced the horse – 'the donkey of the mountains' – from the northern grasslands, and rode to victory in war chariots.

❏ The Babylonians invented many of the number concepts we use, such as changing a number's value by moving it left (in their system this multiplied it by 60, not by 10). Because they counted in twelves we have a 24-hour day and 60-second minute; their 'lucky number' seven led them to devise the seven-day week.

❏ The Babylonians worshiped many gods, often of Sumerian origin. Their chief god was Marduk (below), whose cult center was at Babylon, 'gate of the god.' The cult of Marduk absorbed many other gods – including Sumerian creator-god Enlil – to make him 'the god of fifty names'.

The double crown of Egypt

In Egypt, a great state was founded on the River Nile's fertile black mud – which earned the land the name of 'the Black Country.' Civilization grew up first around the Nile Delta (the Lower Kingdom) and later in the Nile Valley (the Upper Kingdom). Egypt soon acquired irrigation, the plow, and writing, in the form of the famous hieroglyphic picture-script. In c.3100 B.C. King Menes of Upper Egypt conquered the Lower Kingdom, uniting the land under a double crown: the white crown of Upper Egypt and the red crown of Lower Egypt. Menes founded the First Dynasty of Egyptian kings, and built the city of Memphis as his capital. The next 3,000 years saw 31 royal dynasties. Despite intermittent civil wars, when provincial rulers challenged the Memphis dynasties, Egypt enjoyed three periods of stable, prosperous government: the Old (c.2575-2134), Middle (c.2040-1640), and New (c.1550-1070) Kingdoms. This stability owed much to the synthesis of government and religion under kings who were believed to be living gods. A most important part of Egyptian religion was belief in a life after death. This led the country's rulers to spend a fortune on the trappings of death, and produced perhaps the world's most famous royal tombs. These were first built in the period of the Old Kingdom, which is sometimes called the 'Pyramid Age.' Successive kings built pyramids of increasing splendor, culminating in the Great Pyramid of Cheops (Khufu) – one of the Seven Wonders of the Ancient World. The Middle Kingdom saw further great building projects: its new capital of Thebes was glorified with Egypt's largest temple, at Karnak.

Cheops' Great Pyramid at Gizeh took 50,000 workmen the whole of his 23-year reign to build – understandably, since it has c.2.3 million limestone blocks, each weighing 2.5-15 tons.

The pharaoh's grave furnishings included wooden figurines depicting his servants and slaves about their many tasks, like these two busy potters.

A colossal statue of Ramses II 'the Great' dominates his temple at Karnak. This was only one of his immense building projects – perhaps built by the Hebrews in their 'hard bondage.'

Egypt's wealth was 'the gift of the Nile,' whose annual floods brought water and a mud top-dressing to fields in both the marshy delta of Lower Egypt, and the narrow river valley of Upper Egypt.

MEDITERRANEAN SEA

Rosetta
Alexandria
Cairo
Giza
Saqqara
Memphis
LOWER EGYPT
River Nile
Tel-el-Amarna
RED SEA
Karnak
Thebes (Luxor)
UPPER EGYPT
Aswan
Abu-Simbel

FACT FILE

❏ The title 'pharaoh,' adopted during the New Kingdom, means 'great house' – just as we sometimes refer to the U.S. presidency as 'the White House.'

❏ The Egyptians called their script 'the god's word:' we use the Greek term hieroglyph, 'sacred carved inscription.' Hieroglyphics (above) are picture-signs, representing sounds. Later, scribes developed simplified forms – called hieratic and demotic – for everyday use: the detailed hieroglyphic script was kept for formal inscriptions.

❏ Pyramids developed from earlier mastabas (huge brick tombs with sloping sides) when, in c.2620 B.C., King Zoser chose an innovatory design: a stack of six mastabas of decreasing size forming a step-sided pyramid – in durable stone, not brick. His successors perfected the true pyramid, filling in the steps to form smooth sides.

❏ It was probably during the Middle Kingdom that Abraham brought his people into Egypt because of famine in Canaan.

The 'Shepherd Kings'

Egypt's prosperous Middle Kingdom was finally toppled by a mysterious Semitic people (or peoples) from the north, called the Hyksos ('Shepherd Kings'). Many of these foreigners had achieved high office in Egypt; at last they replaced the native rulers and took control of the country. Biblical events are hard to date, but many scholars believe it was during this period that Joseph entered Egypt as a slave and rose to high office. Hyksos pharaohs held Egypt for perhaps a century. During their reigns the wandering Hebrews, previously despised as 'uncivilized' by Egyptian rulers, enjoyed security, tending their flocks and herds in the Nile Delta. Later a new dynasty from Upper Egypt adopted Hyksos military technology – the horse and chariot, bronze weapons, and the powerful composite bow – and successfully turned it on the foreign rulers. The Hyksos kings were expelled from Egypt, and the victorious generals founded the New Kingdom. Egypt's new military strength was deployed to expand the realm into Palestine and Syria. In a reign lasting some 54 years, Thutmose III led a series of campaigns against the Canaanites. In c.1479 B.C. his highly-organized army of some 10,000 men drove the Canaanite forces back to the fortified town of Megiddo, and took it after a siege lasting seven months. The battle established Egyptian control over the land of Canaan (Palestine). The site of Megiddo (near modern Haifa) is sometimes said to be the 'Armageddon' where, according to the biblical Book of Revelations, the last great battle between good and evil will be fought.

Modern Bedouins follow the same lifestyle as Hebrew patriarchs Abraham, Isaac, and Jacob: tent-dwellers who drive their flocks and herds from pasture to pasture.

Egyptian portrayal of Semites bearing tribute. Native Egyptians despised nomadic herders – 'sand-dwellers.' Only under the foreign Hyksos rulers were the Semites welcomed in Egypt.

Sethos I charges into battle against the Libyans. New Kingdom pharaohs learned from the Hyksos rulers and adopted the iron-wheeled war chariot, the latest thing in military technology.

Joseph's brothers, fed up with their father's pet, sell him to slavers – and make his fortune. In Egypt he rose to power – as did many Semites under the Hyksos rulers.

Egypt's horses were too small to equip mounted cavalry – but, harnessed in pairs, provided later pharaohs with highly effective chariot corps.

The Egyptian artist shows Libyans – in fact skilled archers – as helpless before the pharaoh's chariot.

FACT FILE

❏ The Egyptians preserved their dead by mummification to ensure a physical resurrection. The Israelite Joseph was embalmed, a departure from Hebrew practice which shows how his people had integrated into Egypt's society.

❏ Jacob, Joseph's father, gave the Hebrews a new title. He took the name of Israel, and his people became the Israelites.

❏ The Hebrews probably acquired the custom of circumcision from the Egyptians, who instituted this practice. The Greek writer Herodotus, who visited Egypt in c.450 B.C., tells us they did so 'for the sake of cleanliness, considering it better to be cleanly than comely.'

❏ Thutmose III (below) was an outstanding military leader who did not shirk personal danger. In the attack on Megiddo he led his army down a narrow track, 'his Majesty showing the way by his own footsteps.' It is recorded that his bodyguard Amenemhab saved his life on two occasions: once in battle, and once from a herd of wild elephants in Syria.

The Hebrews enslaved

The pharaoh was not only royal but divine: when he died he would take his rightful place among the gods. Here Ramses III is welcomed by the goddess Isis.

Not content with expelling the Hyksos rulers, the New Kingdom pharaohs clamped down on all foreigners remaining within Egypt's borders. Exodus tells us: 'there arose up a new king over Egypt, which knew not Joseph,' and describes how Pharaoh made the Israelites labor 'in mortar, and in brick, and in all manner of service in the field,' and build 'treasure cities, Pithom and Raamses.' Biblical scholars have failed to identify the pharoah concerned, but the mighty Ramses II (c.1301-1234 B.C.) is a strong candidate. His reign saw unprecedented building works, and the Biblical city of Raamses may have been his new capital, Per-Ramesses, where he raised a massive temple and a luxurious palace, inlaid with gold, silver, lapis lazuli, and turquoise. At Abu Simbel (Nubia) he ordered a vast temple cut out of the rocks overlooking the Nile. His statue at the Ramesseum, his mortuary temple at Luxor, was the biggest ever carved in Egypt. It weighed c.1,000 tons 907 tonnes and was cut from a single piece of stone in the quarries of Aswan some 150mi (240km) away: not only its carving, but its transport to Luxor was a miracle of ancient technology. Such projects required a huge workforce of slave labor – while for lesser buildings an immense quantity of sun-dried bricks was needed. It was at brick-making, Exodus tells us, that the Israelites spent their years of bondage, until the combination of a forceful Hebrew leader, Moses, and a series of disasters, the 'plagues' of the Bible, persuaded Pharaoh to release them.

Semitic captives in Egypt – where foreigners were considered fit only for slavery – and indeed Egypt's wealth relied on plentiful slave labor.

❏ Pharaoh Ramses II (below) had more than 90 wives and more than 100 sons. Examination of his mummy reveals that, when he died in his late eighties, he also had severe arthritis, advanced heart disease, and bad teeth.

❏ Brickmakers mixed their mud or clay with straw, to allow firing of bricks with minimal fuel before the fierce sun finished the process. The Hebrews were punished for rebellion by being made to gather their own straw instead of having it supplied. From this comes our saying, 'to make bricks without straw' – to work without vital materials.

❏ Some scholars see the plagues of Egypt, which persuaded Pharaoh to release the Hebrews, as the results of a major volcanic eruption – perhaps that of the Mediterranean island of Thera in c.1450 B.C.

Death mask of Tutankhamun: in life a minor New Kingdom pharaoh, today famous since his tomb escaped graverobbers and his treasures survive.

Painted chest from Tutankhamun's tomb. Egyptian religion was quite clear that 'you can take it with you when you die.'

33

The wandering Jews

To this day Jews honor the anniversary of the Exodus (literally 'going out'), their forebears' departure from Egypt, some 3,300 years ago, for the land promised by God. It was to be a long, hard journey. Moses led his people south towards the wilderness of the Sinai peninsula, avoiding a more direct northern route through dangerous Philistine territory. Pursued by Egyptian soldiers, the fleeing Israelites came to a 'sea,' identified by the early translators of the Bible as the Red Sea (Gulf of Suez), but thought by some to be a lake called the Reed Sea, perhaps on the route of the modern Suez Canal. The Bible tells how God parted the sea for the Israelites to cross dryfoot; then the waters returned, drowning their pursuers. The Sinai wilderness which they had to cross was bleak indeed after Egypt's plenty, yet capable of sustaining nomadic herders, as it does to this day. For 40 years it sustained the Israelites; the Bible describes how they found food in this apparent desert, from flocks of quails to the miraculous manna. Somewhere in this land they came to Mount Sinai. The actual site has never been identified with certainty, but at this holy place a covenant was struck between God and His people, with a set of moral laws (the Ten Commandments) which has formed the basis of both the Jewish and the later Christian faiths. The stone tablets on which the Commandments were carved were kept in a chest of acacia wood and gold, the Ark of the Covenant – the Israelites' most sacred possession.

The Israelites were never to forget the hardships of the Sinai desert, where they wandered seeking grazing for their flocks and herds – and water, for survival.

A miracle in the desert: at God's command, Moses strikes a rock and water gushes forth, restoring the Israelites' confidence.

Traditionally, painters depict Moses with horns – they should be rays of light, but English Bible translators made a mistake!

The Ark of the Covenant, a portable shrine, answered the Israelites' need for a tangible symbol of their abstract God.

Canaan: the promised land

When the Israelites reached Canaan it was still technically under Egyptian rule. In fact the land was held by a number of tribes – Amalekites, Amorites, Canaanites, Hittites, and Jebusites – who guarded their territory with recently developed iron weapons, and whose cities were surrounded by walls. But most of these 'cities,' that at first so impressed the tent-dwelling Israelites, were little more than fortified villages, already declining from their Bronze Age peak. Inter-tribal warfare had prevented political unity and had left Canaan vulnerable to invasion. The Israelites had yet to develop iron and were still using less durable bronze weapons, but they had the advantage of strong leadership, under Moses and his successor Joshua, and faith in their cause. Moses led the first victorious campaigns against the Amorites and Moabites, and in c.1230 B.C. the Israelites stood on the banks of the Jordan River, ready to invade. Here Moses died. Joshua took over, leading the Israelites across the Jordan to attack the ancient city of Jericho, which fell after a siege (its walls, according to the Bible, crumbling at the sound of the Israelites' 'trumpets' and warcries). The Israelites went on to capture other towns, including Schechem, Lachish, and Hazor, whose ruins preserve evidence of destruction by fire at this period. By 1200 B.C. Canaan was theirs and settlement began, with allocation of territory to each of the tribes of Israel. Conquest was not total: the Canaanites still held parts of the land, along with some major cities like Jerusalem, and the Israelites would have to fight to establish and retain their Promised Land.

The land of Canaan. The Israelites took their promised land by conquest; thereafter, this small country was to be a bone of contention in power struggles between great nations.

MEDITERRANEAN SEA

River Jordan

Megiddo

Jericho

Jerusalem

Hebron

DEAD SEA

These rounded shapes may represent worshipers; one (right) features two arms raised in prayer towards a moon symbol.

Finds from a Canaanite temple to the moon god at Hazor: a seated figure, and a group of carved slabs (*stelae*). Some Israelites were drawn to Canaanite religion, a defection which was roundly condemned by later prophets.

The Canaanite city of Lachish was occupied by the Israelites for 600 years. This tel (mound) marks the site: excavation of its layers revealed ten successive periods of settlement.

❏ The name Canaan means 'Land of the Purple' – the highly-prized purple dye made from shellfish caught off the Phoenician coast.

❏ Jericho's walls (above) were rebuilt 19 times over many centuries. At their strongest they were some 23ft (7m) high, 6ft (2m) thick, and 880yd (800m) in extent, with a moat about 27ft (8.2m) wide and 9ft (2.7m) deep. Archeologists have found no trace of Joshua's conquest: it seems the city was deserted before the Israelites came. Some scholars think wind and rain destroyed signs of later occupation; or that Joshua's Jericho was elsewhere; or that the story of Jericho's fall was invented to explain the ruins.

❏ Once settled, the Israelites adopted much of the local Canaanite culture, abandoning their tents to build brick houses, often in the ruins of the towns they had destroyed. But one group of diehards, the Rechabites, believed only the old nomadic lifestyle was acceptable to God. They remained tent-dwelling herdsmen, shunning all refinements unknown in the desert, from wine to razors.

Mountain warriors: the Hittites

A gold statuette, 1.7in (4.2cm) high, from the 14th century B.C., shows a man in full-sleeved tunic and conical hat – perhaps a Hittite king.

The Hittites arrived in Asia Minor before 2000 B.C., perhaps from Europe or southern Russia. Around 1750, under Hattusilas I, Hittite states united to form an empire, with its capital at Hattusas, a natural fortress in the Anatolian mountains (modern Turkey). War chariots and a virtual monopoly of iron gave the Hittites military superiority over their neighbors. Within a century, their empire extended into Syria, and in 1590 they sacked Babylon, leaving Mesopotamia divided between rival peoples. Not long afterwards the Hittites fell into eclipse, but in c.1380 they rose again, greater than before, and gained domination over the entire 'Fertile Crescent,' except for Egypt. Under Ramses II, Egypt attempted to win back Syria. In c.1300 Egyptians and Hittites met in the battle of Kadesh. Ramses claimed victory – but the Hittites retained Syria. Soon both united under a common threat from Assyria, and in c.1284 signed a peace treaty, sealed by Ramses' marriage to a Hittite princess. Ramses thereby secured control of Canaan (already under Egyptian occupation). When Moses led the Israelites into Canaan they had to fight the occupying Hittites, as well as other tribes. After Joshua's conquest of Canaan, Hittites remained in the land and intermarried with the Hebrews: the Old Testament records Hittites among David's followers and in Solomon's harem. The Hittite Empire collapsed in c.1200 under attack from invaders from the sea; refugees established city-states in northern Syria, where Hittite culture lingered until crushed by the growing power of Assyria in the 8th century B.C.

Hattusas was protected by a massive wall, 4mi (6.4km) round and in places 8 ft (2.4m) thick. The massive Lion Gate (c.1800 B.C.) guarded the 10ft (3.6m) wide southwest entrance.

Hittite potters made enchanting painted animal-form vessels, combining realism and fantasy, like this two-headed duck.

Once stone sentry towers and double bronze-plated wooden gates assisted the great carved lions to protect the gateway of Hattusas.

Another animal-form vessel – this time a bird whose three legs give it more stability than a realistic two. The long tail forms the spout.

Bronze animal-form standard from the Royal Tombs of Alaca Huyuk. The site yielded many of these 'standards,' which were probably mounted on poles.

❏ The vast sanctuary of Yazilikaya, outside the city walls of Hattusas, was the religious center of the Hittite empire. The first temple was built there in c.1460 B.C.; later, spectacular reliefs of the gods were carved in the rock face. Above: King Tudhaliyash IV, with the symbol for divinity.

❏ Hittite leader Muwatallis successfully ambushed Ramses' troops at Kadesh, after pretending to have abandoned the city. His 2,500 war chariots destroyed a division of Ramses' army, leaving survivors in disarray. The Egyptians rallied, but won the day only when reserve troops arrived from the coast. Ramses' victory was not decisive: Kadesh – and Syria – remained in Hittite hands.

❏ Thousands of cuneiform tablets survive from the Hattusas state archives: royal edicts, treaties with foreign powers, official letters – and 'dictionaries' translating Babylonian and Sumerian into the Hittite language.

Peoples of the sea

On the coastal strip of modern Israel and Lebanon, from 1500 B.C., the Phoenicians founded a great civilization on sea trade. Their ships sailed remarkable distances – according to Greek historians, even circumnavigating Africa in a three-year voyage – and their farflung colonies included the major cities of Tyre, Sidon, and Byblos (all in modern Lebanon), and Carthage (Tunisia). Between 1200-1150 the Phoenicians joined an alliance of tribes, the Sea Peoples, whose raids terrorized the eastern Mediterranean. The Sea Peoples destroyed the Hittite Empire, but their attempt to invade Egypt was repelled by Ramses II in c.1190. Egyptian carvings portraying Ramses' victory show the Sea Peoples' warships with sails, their war chariots, round shields, and long broadswords, and the ox-carts which carried supplies and their armies' families. After their defeat in Egypt, the Sea Peoples settled in Palestine. One group, the Philistines, annexed the Canaanite coast, establishing a league of five cities: Gaza, Ashkelon, Ashdod, Ekron, and Gath. When the Israelites settled in Canaan, the Philistines became their chief enemy. The Old Testament records many Philistine-Israelite clashes, such as the story of Samson, champion of the tribe of Dan. Only under the first Israelite kings, Saul and David (who first achieved fame by slaying the giant Philistine warrior Goliath), was the Philistine threat repelled after a series of major battles. From their own coastal territory, the Philistines maintained their independence for centuries, causing occasional disturbances in later times.

The anthropoid (human-shaped) coffin of Phoenician King Eshmunazar is a portrait of the dead monarch. Later, Philistine coffins show a simplified design.

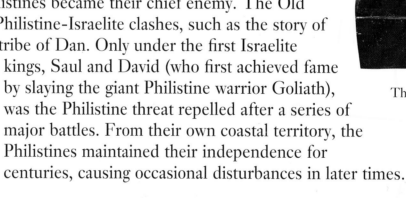

Phoenicians

Philistines

Byblos

Sidon   Damascus

Tyre

Hazor

Ekron

Ashdod   Jerusalem

Gaza   Ashkelon

Phoenician territory (shaded green on the map) centred around Byblos, Sidon, and Tyre. The Philistines founded cities farther south down the coast.

An early picture of one of the trading ships – made of timber from the fabled cedars of Lebanon – that made the Phoenicians masters of the ocean. They depended mainly on sail, with a long steering oar on the port side.

The great Canaanite city of Ashkelon, covering 136 acres (55ha), became a Philistine stronghold – which the hero Samson raided. Today it lies in ruins.

❏ The Phoenician city of Byblos (above) gave its name to our Bible. It was the Phoenicians who invented the alphabet; when the Greeks adopted this invaluable tool they used the name of Byblos – as the source of the alphabet – as their word for a book (*biblos*). This became our word for Christianity's great book, the Bible.

❏ The Old Testament states that the Philistines originated from Crete (Caphtor). This is supported by a study of Philistine pottery, which resembles Mycenaean pottery from Crete and mainland contemporary Greece.

❏ The story of Israelite hero Samson ends with his captivity at the Philistine city of Gaza. Enslaved and blinded, he triumphed at last by pulling down the pillars of the temple: the whole structure fell, killing both Samson and his enemies. Excavation of the ruins of Gaza has revealed the remains of a temple with two wooden pillars supporting the roof.

Rival gods

Fertility figurines from the Israelite period (c.7th-6th century B.C.). These stylized women, with heavy breasts, otherwise sketchy torsos, and no legs, differ little from Stone Age mother goddesses carved some 25,000 years earlier.

The Israelites' loyalty to their belief in one God had to withstand exposure to other nations' polytheism (worship of many gods). Widespread rival cults included those of fertility goddesses like the Egyptian Isis and Phoenician Astarte; the Philistine sea god Dagon; and the many gods of the Canaanite peoples, from sinister Moloch, who demanded child sacrifices, to Baal, worshiped as a rain god who made the land fertile. The Israelites sometimes strayed. When they became settled farmers in Canaan, some of them turned from the Lord God of Israel (whom they saw as a god of wandering shepherds) to Canaanite divinities, farmers' gods concerned with crops and harvests; particularly Baal. Sometimes they covered their bets by worshiping both Baal and the God of Israel. Some gradually extended their worship to other deities: Astarte, Baal's consort, goddess of love and war; El, the creator; Atherat, El's consort. They adopted Canaanite religious rites, combining the local harvest festival with their own Feast of the Passover; worshiped Canaanite sacred animals – the snake and bull; and made the Canaanite goddess Athtart ('Lady of Heaven') consort to their own God. Prophets like Jeremiah angrily denounced Baal-worship, but it remained a problem for the Israelite religion for centuries. Israel had to fall, and the Israelites had to endure long exile in Babylon, before the Jewish faith was purified. Then Baal the Thunderer, Lord of the Lofty Dwelling, became the lesser devil Baalzebub (or Beelzebub), Lord of the Flies, chief assistant of Satan.

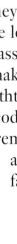

Astarte, Canaanite mother goddess – wife, sister, and perhaps mother to fertility god Baal – was 'the lady of the mountain,' 'the lady of the sea,' and 'queen of heaven.'

Baal, god of fertility, whose myth reflects the cycle of the seasons. He exiled Mot, god of death, was himself summoned by Mot to the land of the dead, and was restored to life by his wife Astarte.

Egyptian god of death Osiris, like Baal, himself suffered death and was resurrected. His cult spread far beyond Egypt as one of the 'mystery religions' that preceded the rise of Christianity.

Babylonian goddess Ishtar required women to have ritual sex with a stranger. Greek historian Herodotus (c.484-425 B.C.) records that pretty women managed easily, but 'the uncomely sometimes have to wait several years.'

❑ Much of our knowledge of the Canaanite gods comes from clay tablets of c.1300 B.C., found at the site of the city of Ugarit, near Latakia in modern Syria.

❑ Hebrew writers accused the Canaanites of such practices as ritual prostitution and child sacrifice. The many infant burials found under Canaanite buildings may prove the latter charge – or may only show that children who died naturally were buried at home.

❑ Each Canaanite city had its own patron deity, often called *baal* or *baalat* ('lord' or 'lady') – not to be confused with the great god Baal, or 'Lord'.

❑ The titles, roles, and attributes of Mesopotamian deities often changed, as nations interacted and one cult influenced another. Thus, the Sumerian fertility goddess Innanna became, in later mythologies, Ishtar, Astarte (below), Cybele, Aphrodite, or Venus. Babylonian Ishtar, goddess of fertility and love, was also 'the lady of battles' – an aspect which the warlike Assyrians accentuated to create a terrible war goddess.

Land of milk and honey

To the Israelites, Canaan was 'a land of milk and honey' after their years in the wilderness. Its rounded hills offered grazing for flocks; grain and fruit could be grown in its fertile valleys. Unlike either Egypt, which depended on great irrigation schemes, or Sinai's bleak desert, Canaan had enough rainfall to support small farmers (today this is true only of the narrow coastal strip). Despite modern development, much of the landscape today is unchanged since Old Testament times. Many biblical sites are identifiable, either by tradition or through archeological detective work. Natural features echo Bible stories: the mountain of Hebron, where Abraham pitched his tents; the Spring of Elisha, which still feeds the oasis of Jericho. The eerie rock salt formations near the Dead Sea recall the fate of Lot's wife, turned to a pillar of salt when she looked back at condemned Sodom. The Carmelite chapel at Mukhraka marks the place where the prophet Elijah routed Baal's priests. Scattered across the landscape, huge mounds called tels mark the sites of ancient cities, rebuilt many times on the same sites. Excavation of Hazor, Israel's largest tel (c.210 acres/85ha), revealed 25 levels of settlement over some 35 centuries, giving evidence of Joshua's conquest and of Solomon's fortified 'chariot city.' Once the capital of the Canaanite king Jabin, Hazor may have housed c.40,000 people before its destruction by the Assyrians (c.8th century B.C.).

Arrived in Canaan, each family was awarded a plot of land to farm. This modern village differs little from early unwalled farming settlements.

Women in Judaea sift wheat in the fields, letting the wind separate the lighter chaff from the grain, just as in Old Testament times.

King Ahab of Israel (c.874-853 B.C.) rebuilt Canaanite cities Hazor and Megiddo with massive defences, like this city gate (reconstructed) from Hazor.

❏ A Muslim mosque now crowns the Cave of Machpela (below), tomb of the patriarchs Abraham, Isaac, and Jacob, and their wives. Herod raised a monument here. The mosque dates from A.D. 638. From the 12th century, non-Muslims were forbidden to enter, but since 1967 members of all religions have been admitted to view the cenotaphs marking the position of the tombs in the cave beneath.

❏ Jerusalem, some 5000 years old, is one of the world's oldest continuously-inhabited cities. At the time of the Israelite settlement it was only a small town, occupying the south-eastern hill of the modern city.

❏ By Jewish tradition, Moses died in the land of Moab, across the Jordan. Muslims (who venerate the biblical patriarchs and prophets, including Jesus among the latter) believe that Allah brought Moses' remains to Nebi Musa, near the Dead Sea, where for centuries his tomb was a pilgrimage center.

❏ Neot Kedumim, a botanical garden near Jerusalem, features every plant mentioned in the Bible and the Talmud.

Jews, Christians, and Muslims alike honor monuments like Rachel's Tomb, Bethlehem – where women pray, like Jacob's wife Rachel, for a child.

Of vital importance, sheep provided meat, milk, wool, leather, ramshorn for flasks and trumpets – and 'clean' beasts for sacrifice.

45

King David of Israel

The story of David and Goliath, in medieval stained glass.

David's first great exploit: a humble shepherd boy, he lays low Philistine champion Goliath with a boy's weapon, the humble slingshot, and cuts off his head.

Once settled in Canaan, the 12 tribes of Israel exchanged the national leadership of Moses and Joshua for a tribal society. They relied on local war-leaders (the 'Judges' of the Bible) to fend off their foes. But constant threats from Ammonites, Canaanites, Midianites, Moabites, and Philistines later made central leadership a necessity. It took the form of a monarchy: in c.1000 B.C., Saul was crowned first king of Israel. He won battles with the Ammonites, Amalekites, and Philistines, but it was his successor, David, who established Israel as a great nation. David began his career in Saul's service, when he killed the Philistine champion Goliath, but was exiled when Saul grew jealous of his military success. David fled to outlawry in the mountains of Ein Gedi, near the Dead Sea, and later entered the service of the Philistines under Achish, king of Gath. Saul's death in battle with the Philistines on the slopes of Mount Gilboa left Israel in disarray. Saul's son Ishbosheth became the ineffectual king of the northern part of the territory; but Israel's salvation lay in the south, at Hebron, where the elders of Judah crowned David as king. From Judah, he gradually won control of the whole country and united the 12 tribes. He went on to defeat Israel's old enemies and expand the kingdom, taking in the lands of Edom, Moab, and Ammon on the east bank of the Jordan. His capture of the Jebusite stronghold of Jerusalem gave Israel a new, central capital. When he died, after a reign of 40 years, he left a strong, secure, and peaceful kingdom.

Ruins of Beth-shean, a city which resisted the Israelite invasion but fell to the Philistines – who later displayed on its walls the bodies of Saul and his son Jonathan, David's dear friend.

From a precarious beginning at Hebron, David went on to control a kingdom which united Israel and Judah and extended influence northward, controlling major land and sea trade routes.

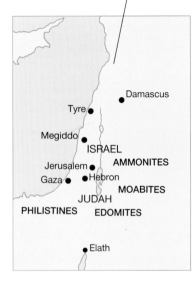

Damascus

Tyre

Megiddo

ISRAEL

Jerusalem AMMONITES

Gaza Hebron

MOABITES

JUDAH

PHILISTINES EDOMITES

Elath

This grave in Jerusalem, not 'King David's Tomb' on nearby Mount Zion (for 800 years a pilgrimage site), may be David's resting place.

❑ In c.1050 B.C., the Philistines captured the Ark of the Covenant at the battle of Eben-ezer. When plague and disaster struck them, they blamed this on the wrath of Israel's God. In desperation, they returned the Ark – with an offering of five golden mice; perhaps the role of rats and mice as plague-carriers was already suspected. For the next 20 years the Ark was kept safely at Kirjath-jearim, until David brought it to Jerusalem.

❑ In Saul's time, the Philistines retained a monopoly on iron. Under David, Israel acquired from them both the use of iron, and a new vocabulary – Hebrew words for 'knife' and 'helmet' are both borrowings from the Philistine language.

❑ David made the Israelite army a crack fighting force by learning military strategy from his enemies. He is remembered not only as a great leader, but also as a lover of music. He played the *kinnor* (a small harp or lyre) (above) and the *nebel* or psaltery (a larger stringed instrument), and is credited with 73 of the songs of the Book of Psalms.

Jerusalem, the holy city

Jerusalem has many monuments of Old and New Testament days, including the so-called Tomb of Absalom.

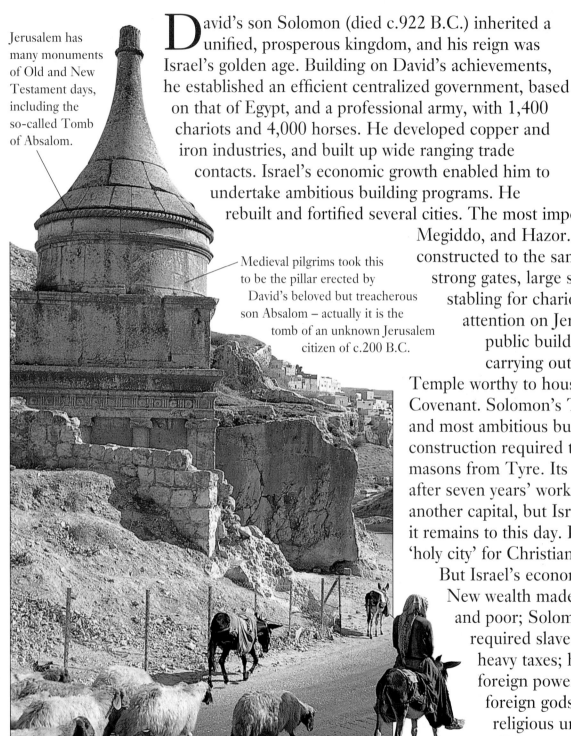

Medieval pilgrims took this to be the pillar erected by David's beloved but treacherous son Absalom – actually it is the tomb of an unknown Jerusalem citizen of c.200 B.C.

David's son Solomon (died c.922 B.C.) inherited a unified, prosperous kingdom, and his reign was Israel's golden age. Building on David's achievements, he established an efficient centralized government, based on that of Egypt, and a professional army, with 1,400 chariots and 4,000 horses. He developed copper and iron industries, and built up wide ranging trade contacts. Israel's economic growth enabled him to undertake ambitious building programs. He rebuilt and fortified several cities. The most important were Gezer, Megiddo, and Hazor. All three were constructed to the same plan, with double walls, strong gates, large storage buildings, and stabling for chariotry. Above all, he lavished attention on Jerusalem, raising splendid public buildings and palaces, and carrying out his father's plan to erect a Temple worthy to house the Ark of the Covenant. Solomon's Temple was Israel's largest and most ambitious building to date; its construction required the import of skilled masons from Tyre. Its completion in c.950 B.C., after seven years' work, made Jerusalem not just another capital, but Israel's religious center – as it remains to this day. Later it would become a 'holy city' for Christians and Muslims as well.

But Israel's economic boom had its price. New wealth made a division between rich and poor; Solomon's building program required slave and forced labor, and heavy taxes; his marriage-alliances with foreign powers brought the worship of foreign gods to Israel, weakening the religious unity of the people. Discontent grew among the Israelites, paving the way for the division of the kingdom after Solomon's death.

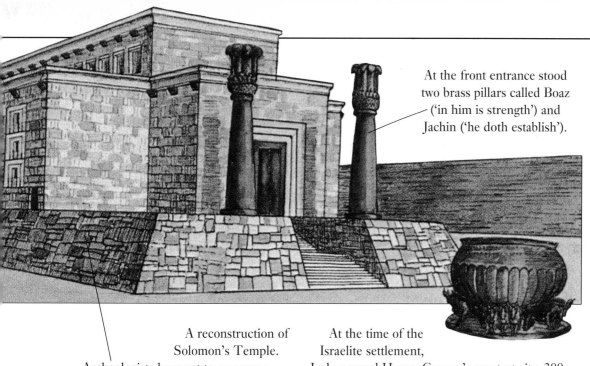

At the front entrance stood two brass pillars called Boaz ('in him is strength') and Jachin ('he doth establish').

A reconstruction of Solomon's Temple. Archeologists have yet to uncover a temple like it, but a Canaanite shrine at Hazor has a similar three-room plan.

At the time of the Israelite settlement, Joshua razed Hazor, Canaan's greatest city. 300 years later Solomon rebuilt it as one of his great regional military and administrative centers.

FACT FILE

❑ Inside Solomon's Temple, finely-dressed stonework was hidden by carved cedar paneling overlaid with gold. A hall led to a shrine with an incense altar, *menorah* (ritual candlesticks), and a table for the Sabbath offering of shew-bread (12 new loaves, one for each tribe). Beyond lay the inner sanctum, the Holy of Holies, housing the Ark. Only priests entered the temple: the public sacrificed in the outer courtyard.

❑ Solomon's Temple was destroyed by Babylonians in 587 B.C. It was rebuilt on a lesser scale by Zerubbabel in c.515, and again destroyed by the Romans in 63 B.C. Its site is now occupied by the 'Wailing Wall' (remains of a later temple, built by Herod) – a place of pilgrimage, where Jews mourn the Temple's destruction.

❑ Trade brought new luxuries for the wealthy – Solomon imported gold, silver, ivory, jewels, spices, fine timber, peacocks, and other exotic creatures. It also brought visitors: the legendary Queen of Sheba (southwest Arabia), traveled c.1,000mi (1,600km) by camel caravan to Jerusalem, perhaps as part of a trade delegation. Horse and chariot trade between Asia Minor and Egypt filled Solomon's coffers – and stables: today the Kehilan strain of Arab horse is said to descend directly from his stallion Zad er Rakib.

Assyrian splendor

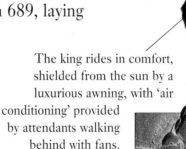

This finely-carved ivory plaque from Ashurbanipal's palace at Nimrud is Phoenician work – probably loot from a Phoenician city.

In the 8th century B.C. 'the Assyrian came down like a wolf on the fold.' A succession of empire-building kings led the Assyrian army – the first to make full use of iron weapons and body armor – to triumph across the Middle East. The Assyrians were a Semitic people, settled in northwest Mesopotamia by 2300 B.C. Their first great state (c.1500-1100) fell to Aramaean invaders, to be followed by 150 years of obscurity. Then military genius Ashurnasirpal II (reigned 883-859) built his army into an unbeatable fighting force and won an empire running from the Mediterranean to the Persian Gulf, and extending into Upper Egypt. Tribute from conquered lands went to build his splendid capital at Nimrud. Assyria's hold on its subject kingdoms was confirmed by Tiglath-pileser III (reigned 745-727), whose skilfull organization of provincial government brought Babylonia, Palestine, Syria, and Phoenicia firmly under Assyrian control, and by Sennacherib (reigned 705-681), who crushed a Babylonian revolt in 689, laying waste Babylon itself. Sennacherib moved his capital to Nineveh, where his vast building program outdid Nimrud in splendour. His son Esarhaddon (reigned 681-669) quelled rebellion in Egypt and Phoenicia, and rebuilt Babylon. But Assyria's empire became too large for effective control. Ashurbanipal (reigned 669-627) was forced to withdraw from Egypt, and soon after his death a strong Babylonian ruler, Nabopolassar, won independence for Babylon in 625. In alliance with the Medes, Babylon rose against Assyria. In 612 they destroyed Nineveh, and the mighty Assyrian Empire came to an end.

The king rides in comfort, shielded from the sun by a luxurious awning, with 'air conditioning' provided by attendants walking behind with fans.

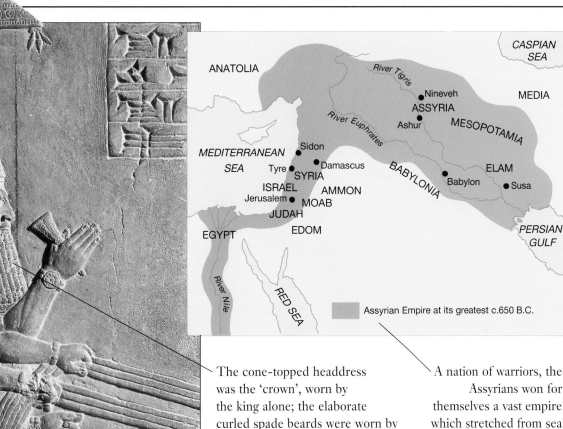

Assyrian Empire at its greatest c.650 B.C.

The cone-topped headdress was the 'crown', worn by the king alone; the elaborate curled spade beards were worn by most Assyrians – supplemented by 'chin wigs' on state occasions.

A nation of warriors, the Assyrians won for themselves a vast empire which stretched from sea to sea – and eventually became too much to hold.

❑ Ashurnasirpal's palace at Nimrud displayed his wealth and power, with huge alabaster sculptures and lifesize wall-carvings of battles and court ceremonies. Its completion was marked by a ten-day feast, at which (according to records carved on stone) 69, 574 people paid homage to the king.

❑ At Nineveh, Sennacherib built temples, magnificent city gates, the 'palace without a rival' (above), and a city water supply via canal and the first 300yd (275m) aqueduct.

❑ The Assyrians ruled by terror. They quelled defeated foes with massacres, mutilation, and mass deportation, and razed their cities, temples, and royal tombs – even their fields, sown with salt to become deserts. Ashurbanipal made captured kings draw his chariot around Nineveh, and spread soil from their towns at his gates to be trodden underfoot.

❑ Ashurbanipal valued learning, as well as war. His library at Nineveh held more than 25,000 works of literature, history, science, math, and medicine – all the knowledge of the world at that time.

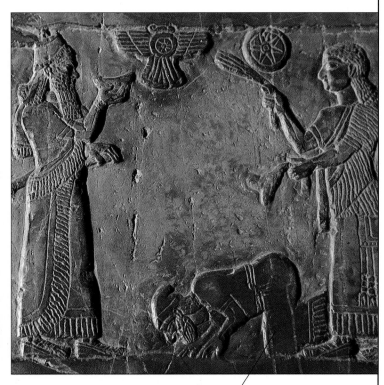

Jehu, King of Israel, pays homage to the conquering Assyrian king Shalmaneser III (858-824 B.C.). The winged sun at the top symbolizes the Assyrian war god Ashur.

By the waters of Babylon

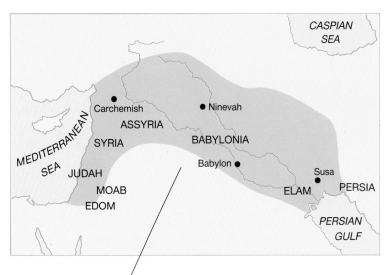

Nebuchadrezzar's Empire at its peak was larger than the earlier Assyrian Empire of Ashurbanipal. When his expansionist drive took in Judah, Jewish prophets like Jeremiah saw him as instrument of God's wrath.

King Nabopolassar's reign in Babylon brought the Chaldeans to power. This Semitic people established the New Babylonian Empire (626-539 B.C.). Nabopolassar's son, Nebuchadrezzar II (604-562) rebuilt the city of Babylon in splendor, creating the famed 'Hanging Gardens.' For processions honoring the god Marduk, he created the most impressive street of the ancient world, the Processional Way – a 1,310yd (1200m) avenue flanked by carved lions. For the goddess Ishtar, he raised the Ishtar Gate, a magnificent gateway of glazed tiles, decorated with 150 bulls and dragons.

He extended his father's empire over the Middle East – and went on to destroy Jerusalem. After Solomon's death, the kingdom of Israel had divided. Ten tribes had formed the Northern Kingdom (Israel), with its capital at Samaria. In 722 Sargon II of Assyria had conquered Israel and deported its people. Israel became the Assyrian province of Samaria, and the ten tribes vanished from history. Two tribes formed the Southern Kingdom (Judah), whose capital was Jerusalem. Judah survived as long as it paid tribute to Babylon, but when King Jehoiakim switched allegiance to Egypt, Nebuchadrezzar II invaded. In 587, after an 18-month siege, he captured and razed Jerusalem. He deported most Judaeans, many to Babylon, where they spent nearly 50 years in exile. The 'Babylonian captivity' was a key period in the history of the Israelites – or, as they now became, the Jews (people of Judah). Only now, when the Jewish state was lost and the people turned for comfort to the religion of Judah, was their national identity truly established.

Babylon's city gates and the walls of the great Processional Way were faced with vividly colored glazed bricks depicting royal heraldic beasts.

Mighty ruins of the Ishtar Gate – once glazed in bright blue, with 150 *mushrushus* (Babylon's dragon) and bulls, alternately white and yellow.

The animal decoration was modeled from a single clay panel, then cut up into bricks, glazed, fired, and reassembled on the walls.

❑ In the 1980s-90s a determined attempt has been made to recreate the splendor of old Babylon. The Iraqi dictator Saddam Hussein has expended huge sums in 'reconstructions' of the Processional Way and Ishtar Gate – now glorifying himself rather than the ancient gods. Whether he will survive long enough to rebuild the 'Hanging Gardens' is questionable.

❑ Under the Assyrian threat, King Hezekiah secured Jerusalem's water supply ready for a siege. The city's source of water, the Gihon Spring, lay outside the city wall, so a tunnel (below) was cut through the rock to bring water from the spring to the Pool of Siloam in Jerusalem. The workmen carved an inscription, recording how two gangs of miners, one working from each end, managed to meet in the middle when a crack in the rock allowed them to hear each others' pickaxes.

The Medes and Persians

Following their successful alliance with Babylon against Assyria, the Medes set about building up their own considerable empire. In 549 B.C. their King Astyages was overthrown by his Persian son-in-law Cyrus the Great, who united Medes and Persians in the Achaemenid Empire (named for the founder of his line), taking the Medes' capital Ecbatana (modern Hamadan, Iran) as his chief city. He went on to conquer more kingdoms – at last creating the world's largest empire up to that time. In 539 Cyrus took Babylon, toppling the Babylonian Empire – some 50 years after the Jewish captivity there had begun. In contrast to Babylon's policy of mass deportation, Cyrus controlled his empire by leaving local rulers in charge of the provinces. In 538 he issued a decree ending the Jewish exile. The Jews could now return home, with most of their Temple treasures, to rebuild Solomon's Temple at Jerusalem. Not all wished to leave Babylon, where they had been free to keep their own religion and customs, and to find employment (many achieving high positions); but more than 40,000 elected to do so. Cyrus's successors maintained his enlightened government, although any revolt was quickly and brutally quelled. The empire grew in wealth under rulers like Darius the Great (548-486) and Xerxes I (c.519-465) – as witnessed by the splendid ruins of the later capitals, Susa and Persepolis. But in 333 the Achaemenids faced the 'conqueror of the world,' Alexander the Great of Macedon. He routed the huge army of Darius III at the battle of Issus, burned Persepolis, and absorbed the Persian Empire into his own vast but short-lived imperial splendor.

It was Darius, continuing Cyrus's generous policy toward subject peoples, who encouraged the Jews to complete the rebuilding of Jerusalem's second Temple.

A relief from the magnificent palace of King Darius the Great at Persepolis portrays a Mede ambassador paying homage to the king, with a pair of Persian courtiers in attendance.

❏ Cyrus built a 1,700mi (2,735km) network of highways to link up his vast empire. It took his envoys a week to ride the full circuit, collecting remounts at 111 staging posts.

❏ Cyrus's son Cambyses inherited none of his father's greatness. His reign began with the murder of his brother; several costly and often unsuccessful campaigns led him to turn to drunkenness and vice. He killed his sister (and wife) Roxana, and his son, and buried 12 of his nobles alive, shortly before his own death (perhaps by suicide).

❏ The cream of the Persian army formed the emperor's bodyguard, known as the 'Ten Thousand Immortals.' Darius the Great valued these men so highly that they were portrayed on the walls of his palaces, like these archers (above).

❏ Darius the Great and his son Xerxes both faced – and crushed – revolts in Babylon. Darius crucified 3,000 leading citizens; Xerxes, in 482 B.C., not only slew the rebels but largely destroyed the city, razing walls and temples. Babylon never rose again.

The stairs leading to the Audience Hall of Darius's palace at Persepolis are carved with long rows of figures – court officials, royal bodyguards, and subjects bearing tribute.

The Persian Empire founded by Cyrus the Great covered at its peak nearly 2,000,000sq mi (c.5,000,000 sq km). The first 'world empire' fell after 2 centuries to another empire-builder, Alexander the Great.

If visiting emissaries were not impressed by the staircase carvings, they must have been awed when they reached the Hall, which held 10,000 people.

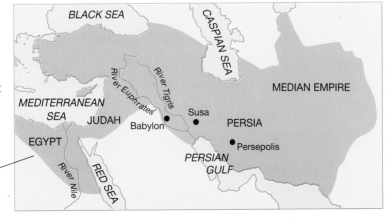

BLACK SEA

CASPIAN SEA

MEDIAN EMPIRE

River Euphrates

River Tigris

MEDITERRANEAN SEA

JUDAH

Babylon

Susa

PERSIA

Persepolis

EGYPT

River Nile

RED SEA

PERSIAN GULF

The Greek kings of Egypt

Alexander's empire did not outlast him: when he died in 323 B.C. his generals shared out his lands. One took Egypt, where as Ptolemy I he founded a line of Greek kings (the Ptolemaic Dynasty) which ruled for 300 years (323-30). He annexed neighboring lands to secure his position and to improve Egypt's domination of the Mediterranean. The library and university he built at Alexandria made that city a cultural hub of the Greek world. Ptolemy II further increased Egypt's power and prestige: his reign produced one of the Seven Wonders of the Ancient World, the Pharos lighthouse at Alexandria. The Ptolemies spread Greek lifestyle, language, and culture among their subject peoples – including the Jews. Judah had been seized by Ptolemy I in 301; more significant was the growing Jewish population in Egypt. Jewish scholars in Alexandria adopted Greek philosophy to create a Hellenistic (Greek-influenced) form of Judaism. They made the first Greek translation of Jewish scriptures. But with the decadent Ptolemy IV (who began his reign by killing his mother and brother), the Greek kings' hold on Egypt faltered. Rome began to reach out for their empire. In 58 B.C. the Alexandrians rebelled against the pro-Roman Ptolemy XI ('the Flute-player'), expelling him from Egypt after he had bought the title of 'friend and ally of Rome.' Another bribe to Rome set him back on the throne in 55. His daughter Cleopatra made an ambitious attempt to restore Ptolemaic greatness (partly through famous love affairs with Julius Caesar and Mark Antony), but with her failure and suicide in 30 B.C. Egypt became a Roman province.

Ptolemy Apion, illegitimate son of Ptolemy VII, ruled Cyrenaica, a small territory northwest of Egypt. He was its last king, for in 98 B.C. he bequeathed his kingdom to Rome.

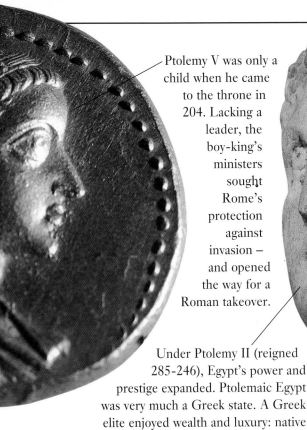

Ptolemy V was only a child when he came to the throne in 204. Lacking a leader, the boy-king's ministers sought Rome's protection against invasion – and opened the way for a Roman takeover.

Under Ptolemy II (reigned 285-246), Egypt's power and prestige expanded. Ptolemaic Egypt was very much a Greek state. A Greek elite enjoyed wealth and luxury: native workers formed a heavily taxed underclass.

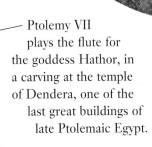

Ptolemy VII plays the flute for the goddess Hathor, in a carving at the temple of Dendera, one of the last great buildings of late Ptolemaic Egypt.

50 years after the death of Alexander the Great, the Seleucids of Syria and Ptolemies of Egypt maintained a vast Greek empire on which they imposed Hellenistic culture.

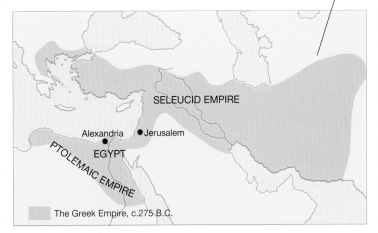

SELEUCID EMPIRE

Alexandria • Jerusalem

EGYPT

PTOLEMAIC EMPIRE

 The Greek Empire, c.275 B.C.

Brothers in arms: the Maccabite rebellion

Antiochus III (223-87), 'the Great,' annexed Judaea as part of the Seleucid Empire, but allowed the Jewish people to keep their own laws and religion.

Like Ptolemaic Egypt, Babylon – soon united with Media and Syria – became a Greek empire in 323 B.C. under one of Alexander the Great's generals, Seleucus, and his heirs. The Seleucid Empire spread Greek culture and language across its realms. Judah (now called in Greek, Judaea) became a Seleucid province in 200. Its new rulers at first tolerated Jewish laws and religion, but later adopted a Hellenizing policy. When this was opposed, Antiochus IV (reigned 175-164) tried to impose Greek culture by force. In 169 he made a savage attack on Jerusalem, butchering many citizens and plundering the Temple, and then set out to crush Judaism entirely. He desecrated the Jews' holy places, banned Sabbath observation and circumcision, and ordered Jews to worship Zeus. Although Jewish society had accepted much Greek influence, and not all Jews opposed Hellenism (those in favor included two ambitious High Priests, Jason and Menelaus), Antiochus's harshness provoked open revolt. The Maccabite Rebellion was begun by the Hasmonean family. Led by Judas Maccabeus ('the Hammerer'), this resistance movement, despite initial lack of numbers and weapons, bested the Seleucid army repeatedly by guerrilla tactics. After four decisive victories, Judas entered Jerusalem in 165 and restored the Temple. After his death in battle five years later, the fight continued. In 142 the last survivor of Judas's four brothers, Simon, won independence for Judaea. He became High Priest, founding the Hasmonean dynasty of priest-rulers under whom Judaea once again extended 'from Dan to Beersheba.'

A romantic engraving by 19th-century artist Gustave Doré shows Judas Maccabeus leading his troops. The bulk of Judas's army was light infantry, but a reference in the *Second Book of Maccabees* suggests development of a small cavalry force.

A medieval view of Antiochus's attack on Jerusalem. Maccabite and Seleucid forces are shown in medieval costume.

Antiochus's men bear off loot. Financially crippled by the tribute imposed by Rome, the Seleucid kings relied on plunder to fund their armies.

Antiochus's Greek fixation led some to change his title *Epiphanes* ('God Manifest'), to *Epimanes* ('the Mad').

Jewish leaders plead for their holy city. But Antiochus was resolved to wipe out Judaism and Hellenize Judaea.

Antiochus ordered a massacre in which 40,000 of the men, women, and children of Jerusalem were killed.

The Nabataeans' 'rose-red city'

The desert region east of Judaea was ruled by the Nabataeans, an Arab people whose nomadic ancestors had moved into south Palestine in the 4th century B.C. They gradually expanded their range, and around the time of Alexander the Great took over the Moabite and Edomite lands, gaining control of important trade routes. Now they adopted a settled life, establishing strongholds from which they taxed camel caravans crossing the desert with luxury goods from Arabia, India, Persia, and China. To support growing settlements, they tamed the desert itself, exploiting its mineral resources, and developing ingenious water catchment systems to grow grain and fruit on terraced land. Their most enduring creation was the 'rose-red city' of Petra (in modern Jordan). A narrow gorge runs for about 1mi (1.6km) between towering cliffs to a city cut from solid rock, with Greek-style villas, palaces, and temples. Petra's vast royal tombs form one of the largest cemeteries of the ancient Middle East; indeed, the city was probably a religious rather than a trade center, for it lay well off the main trade routes. The Nabataeans, strategically placed between the Ptolemaic and Seleucid lands, competed with both, and later took advantage of waning Seleucid power to seize Damascus. The arrival of the Romans in Palestine in 63 B.C. drove them back south, but brought them wealth, as the expanding Roman Empire encouraged trade, and a reviving input of Greek and Roman culture. The last Nabataean king, Rabbel II, died in A.D. 106, and Nabataea became the Roman Emperor Trajan's province of Arabia.

The magnificent Royal Tombs of Petra, cut out of the cliffs east of the city. Below, the so-called 'Palace Tomb.'

The 'Corinthian Tomb' shows the influence of classical architecture. The discovery, in 1812, of this great cemetery in the remote valley of the Wadi Mousa made headlines.

The 'Silk Tomb,' and, right, 'Urn Tomb.'

❏ The world's oldest dental filling was found in the tooth of a Nabataean man buried 2,000 years ago in the Negev Desert. The oldest known dentist seems to have cheated his patient, filling the tooth with corrosive bronze wire instead of gold: this had oxidized, turning the tooth green.

❏ After its sack by Crusaders in the 12th century A.D., Petra lay unknown to the West for c.700 years. Its rediscovery in 1812 by explorer Johann Burckhardt captured popular imagination, inspiring British poet John Burgon's famous description of the 'rose-red city, half as old as time.' Burgon had never seen Petra, which is actually rainbow-hued in every shade of sandstone. Only its monumental Treasury is 'rose-red.'

❏ Green fields and orchards on the site of the Nabataean city of Avdat today (below) mark a modern project proving the worth of ancient irrigation systems. Israeli agriculturists restored parts of the Nabataean irrigation scheme to trap floodwater from the winter rains. Using only primitive farming instruments, they raised good crops in the desert.

Petra's famous Treasury (actually a tomb, but once thought to conceal a pharaoh's gold), stands a towering 100ft (30m) high and 92ft (28m) wide.

The elaborate Greek-style facade is carved out of the solid cliff. Petra means 'rock' – a fitting name for a rock-carved city.

The house of Herod

As the Roman Empire expanded, the independence of Judaea, weakened by quarrels between Hasmonean political and religious factions, was threatened. Julius Caesar's general Pompey the Great took Syria for Rome and moved on Palestine. In 63 B.C., the Judaean princes Hyrcanus II and Aristobulos II asked Pompey to settle their civil war. He did – by making the kingdom a Roman province of three districts (Judaea, Galilee, and Peraea) and appointing Hyrcanus as High Priest. During the Roman Civil War, Hyrcanus and his chief minister Antipater, a Jewish convert of Arab descent, switched allegiance from Pompey to the eventual victor Octavius (later Emperor Augustus). The move was rewarded when Antipater's son, Herod, was appointed client-king of the Jewish state.

Gnaeus Pompeius Magnus, or Pompey the Great (106-48 B.C.), occupied the city of Jerusalem in 63 B.C. and destroyed the second Temple, which had stood for five centuries.

But Herod the Great (reigned 37-4 B.C.) was no puppet: strong and shrewd, well able to manipulate Roman patronage, he ruthlessly eliminated all rivals and established a more powerful (but short-lived) kingdom than the Hasmoneans. He was a great builder, both of fortresses for security and public works – including Jerusalem's new Temple. Under Herod and his heirs, the Jews gained such benefits of Roman civilization as roads and drainage. But they paid dearly in taxes, and Roman rule was widely unpopular. Hope for deliverance focused on the ancient prophesy of Messiah, a king who would save his people. In c.A.D. 27 the prophet John the Baptist announced that Messiah was at hand. John paid with his head for reproving the sins of Herod the Great's son, Herod Antipas – but now the one he had baptized and hailed as Messiah, Jesus Christ, would begin His revolutionary mission.

The ruins of Herod's magnificent palace-fortress of Herodion still command sweeping views over the desert. Herod is said to be buried here, but his mausoleum has never been found.

Over 12 years, Herod upgraded an obscure coastal town to the great city of Caesarea (named for his patron Augustus) – with amphitheater (above), port, hippodrome, and palaces.

Herod's kingdom included most of Palestine, parts of southern Syria, and large areas east of the River Jordan. After his death his three sons divided it.

❏ The chief Jewish religious sects were the Pharisees and Sadducees. Other factions included the Zealots, militant opponents of Roman rule, and the Essenes, isolated even from other Jews by their strictness in observance of religious law.

❏ Herod the Great strengthened his position by marrying Hasmonean princess Mariamne. When she had served her purpose he had her killed (along with other surviving Hasmoneans) and went on to make four further marriages, each bringing political alliances. With equal ruthlessness, he killed several of his sons as possible rivals. Three surviving sons divided his kingdom after his death.

❏ Herod the Great's huge palace-fortresses included Herodion, built on an artificially leveled mountain-top 2,485ft (758m) above sea level and guarded by walls 75ft (23m) high. The palace was built in Greek style – but conforming to the Jewish ban on human images.

❏ John the Baptist condemned Herod Antipas (ruler of Galilee and Peraea, 4 B.C.-A.D. 39) for the religious crime of marrying his sister-in-law, Herodias. Angry Herodias sought John's death and, perhaps, pressured her daughter Salome into demanding the prophet's head from her stepfather (who some said was her lover).

The Dead Sea Scrolls

In 1947 a Bedouin boy pursuing a stray goat entered a cave near the shore of the Dead Sea – and made a discovery that thrilled scholars all over the world. The hoard of leather rolls tucked into old jars did not seem very exciting to the shepherd boy, but it is now renowned as the 'Dead Sea Scrolls,' a collection of documents dating from early New Testament times. Research has identified them as the library of a community of Essenes who lived at Qumran, on the Dead Sea, in the 1st century A.D. The Essene sect was formed during the Maccabite Revolt, as an extremist splinter group from the strict Hasidim ('pious ones'). They deserted the orthodox Jewish community to follow a life of self-denial, hard labor, and dedicated study of Judaic law, in isolated colonies like that at Qumran. Once the value of the first documents found was recognized, archeologists and local people gathered pieces of more than 400 rolls. Written mostly in Hebrew or Aramaic, they include all the books of the Old Testament except Esther. Pre-dating by some 1,000 years the Hebrew version of c.A.D. 900 (previously the oldest known), they prove the faithfulness of later copyists. The texts include descriptions of the Essenes' beliefs and way of life, and tell how the Qumran community, 'Sons of Light', awaited the coming of Messiah. But the community was wiped out by the Roman army in A.D. 68. Only their treasured books survived, hidden as the Roman troops advanced, preserved by the dry desert heat – and now reverently preserved in the Shrine of the Book, at Jerusalem.

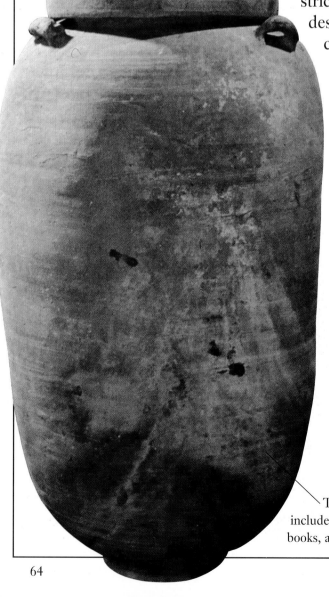

Clay storage jars preserved the fragile leather scrolls – and their rounded lids inspired the domed shape of the modern Shrine of the Book, where the scrolls are kept today.

The contents of these jars included nearly all the Old Testament books, as well as Essene commentaries.

The Isaiah Scroll (17 leather sheets sewn together) is the oldest copy of the Book of Isaiah by 1,000 years – written c.900 years after the time of the prophet Isaiah himself.

The advance of the 'Sons of Darkness' – any enemy to the Essenes, and in this case the Roman army – drove the Qumran community to conceal their 'library' in nearby caves.

❑ Some scholars think John the Baptist may have been a member of the Essene sect. Some suggest that Jesus Himself was an Essene, pointing out that His community of disciples followed Essene standards of self-denial, pacifism, rejection of wealth, and sharing of property.

❑ Excavations at Qumran (above) revealed a large and well-organized settlement. In the scriptorium, or writing room, even the bronze inkwells survive to testify to the scribes' devoted labor.

❑ The title Messiah – 'the anointed one' may mean a spiritual leader or an earthly king. The Essenes of Qumran anticipated two Messiahs, one in each role: 'the Messiah of Aaron,' a priest to restore the true Temple; and the 'Messiah of Israel,' a righteous king.

❑ Some writers alleged that information from the Dead Sea Scrolls has been deliberately suppressed, since to make it public would cause turmoil among Jews and Christians alike. The nature of this 'hidden knowledge' remains a subject of sensational speculation.

A child is born

According to Luke's Gospel, we owe the setting of Jesus Christ's birth (Nativity) in a stable to Roman bureaucracy, which decreed a census that made Mary and Joseph travel from Galilee to their ancestral home in Bethlehem, Judaea. The 'little town of Bethlehem' was indeed small, but not insignificant. It was famous as the burial place of Jacob's wife Rachel, the birthplace of King David – and above all as the prophesied birthplace of Messiah. Today, Israel's oldest surviving church, the Church of the Nativity, stands where Jesus was born. In a grotto beneath the altar, a silver star marks His birthplace; nearby, the Chapel of the Manger honors His humble crib. He was born in the last years of Herod the Great, a time of unrest when many Jews looked for deliverance from Roman rule by the promised Messiah. We are told that Herod responded to rumors of Messiah's birth by ordering all boy babies in Bethlehem to be killed:

In the 4th century Helena, Emperor Constantine's mother, built the first Church of the Nativity at Bethlehem; the present church is 6th-century, with Crusader additions.

the Massacre of the Innocents. The Chapel of St. Joseph, in St. Catherine's Church, Bethlehem, commemorates the site where an angel warned Joseph to flee from this peril and take his family to Egypt. On Herod's death, the Holy Family returned to the Galilean village of Nazareth – their home town, according to Luke's Gospel. There, the vast Basilica of the Annunciation marks a cave venerated for some 1,600 years as the place where the Archangel Gabriel told Mary she was to bear a child; while the Church of St. Joseph stands over an underground chamber identified with Joseph's carpentry workshop. Jesus spent His childhood at Nazareth, and the modern synagogue there is said to occupy the same site as the one He knew.

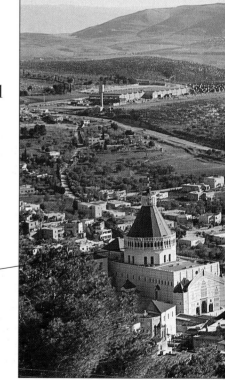

This underground room is held to be the humble home of Mary, where she learned from the Archangel Gabriel that she was to bear a child. Today it is part of Nazareth's Church of the Annunciation.

The modern Church of the Annunciation which dominates Nazareth was consecrated in 1969 – succeeding 5th-century Byzantine, 12th-century Crusader, and 18th-century Franciscan churches.

The Italian Botticelli (c.1445-1510) painted a Renaissance Nativity – including his Medici patrons among the Christ Child's attendants.

The Three Wise Men attend the infant Jesus. Tradition makes them three Kings; but the title Magi suggests they were Persian priests.

❑ Despite our system of numbering years as B.C. (Before Christ) and A.D. (*Anno Domini*; Year of Our Lord), modern researchers set Jesus' birth in A.D. 4. The traditional date of His birth, December 25, was chosen by the Church in A.D. 440, and replaced the pagan winter solstice feast.

❑ The white stone of Bethlehem's Milk Grotto is said to derive from Mary's milk. Today, nursing mothers buy packets of the powdered stone in the belief it will improve their own milk.

❑ The Three Wise Men who attended the infant Jesus are often described as Magi, a Persian priestly caste. Legend says Bethlehem's Church of the Nativity (below) was spared by Persian invaders in 614 because of its portrayal of the Three Wise Men in Persian dress.

❑ The Feast of the Holy Innocents, or Childermas, on December 28, commemorates Herod's massacre of children in Bethlehem. At one time it was the custom to whip children at this feast, to ensure that Herod's crime was duly impressed upon them.

Jesus in Galilee

In c.A.D. 27, when Herod Antipas ruled Galilee and Peraea and the Roman Pontius Pilate ruled Judaea, Jesus began His public ministry by joining the crowds who received baptism in the Jordan from John the Baptist. After John's execution the next year, Jesus returned to His native Galilee. He spent three years as a traveling teacher, with a growing band of followers (Disciples) from whom He chose 12 special companions, the Apostles. Much of this period was spent near or on the Sea of Galilee – Peter and some other Apostles were Galilean fishermen, whom He made 'fishers of men' – but He often visited Jerusalem, and also journeyed into Samaria and to the north. Like other Jewish teachers, He emphasized the personal relationship (Covenant) between God and man. But He rejected the complex religious laws that had built up around the doctrines of Judaism: speaking on His own authority, often by means of tales (parables) in simple language, He reminded people of the spirit of the Law, which had sometimes become hidden by the rigor of its letter. His teachings were accompanied by miracles, which St. John calls 'signs:' healing the sick; feeding 5,000 followers with five loaves and two fishes; even raising the dead. To His followers it was clear that He was indeed Messiah (in Greek, *Christos*). He himself chose the titles 'Servant of God' and 'Son of Man,' to avoid association with the widespread idea of Messiah as a warrior king like David, come to expel the hated Romans and rule Israel. Jesus spoke of a kingdom not of this world, and only at the very end of His ministry did He call Himself Messiah.

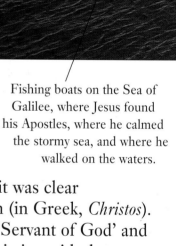

Fishing boats on the Sea of Galilee, where Jesus found his Apostles, where he calmed the stormy sea, and where he walked on the waters.

The synagogue at Cana – a village revered by Christians as the site of Jesus's first miracle. He was attending a marriage party at Cana when the wine ran out, and at his mother's persuasion, turned water to wine to enable celebrations to continue.

The synagogue at Capernaum, the assembly-place where people in Jesus's time met to hear religious teachers – and His Galilee headquarters.

❏ Tabgha, near the Sea of Galilee, has been venerated since the 4th century A.D. as the place of the miracle of the loaves and fishes (above). A site nearby is traditionally held to be where the resurrected Jesus came to His disciples as they fished, and miraculously filled their nets. To this day, shoals of a fish native to the Sea of Galilee (called St. Peter's fish) gather seasonally by Tabgha's warm springs.

❏ Capernaum was the center of Jesus's Galilean ministry. Here and nearby he performed more miracles than anywhere else. But when its people rejected him, he cursed the town: 'And thou, Capernaum, which art exalted unto Heaven, shall be brought down to hell.' Today tourists visit the ruins of this once substantial town.

❏ In a time of unrest, people looked for Messiah in any charismatic leader. Three who claimed to be the Jews' promised savior were Judas of Galilee in 6 A.D.; Theudas in 44 A.D.; and Benjamin the Egyptian in 60 A.D. All three led armed rebellions against Rome, failed, and were crucified. Jesus, who refused the role of war leader, suffered the same death.

Death and Resurrection

Jesus's ministry ended in c.A.D. 30, when He was executed as a common criminal outside Jerusalem's walls. Jewish officials saw His teachings and his popular acceptance as Messiah as blasphemy. They feared public disorder, even revolt, and so did the Roman authorities. On Jesus's last visit to Jerusalem to celebrate Passover, the crowd's welcome and His attack on Temple moneylenders spurred them to act. Fearing that His arrest while among His supporters might provoke a riot, they bribed the Apostle Judas Iscariot to make sure He was taken while praying with a few friends in the Garden of Gethsemane. The Gospels ascribe His death sentence to the Sanhedrin (Jewish court), with the Roman governor Pilate ratifying the sentence only to pacify the Jewish priests. But Rome held power, and many scholars believe the Gospel writers slanted their account to please prospective Roman converts – thus unwittingly laying the foundation for centuries of persecution of Jews by Christians. Although officially condemned for blasphemy, Jesus was crucified, the penalty for rebels against Roman rule. The Via Dolorosa ('Road of Sorrow') traces His route from the place of sentence, the Fortress Antonia, to the place of execution, the side of a quarry outside Jerusalem's walls, now the site of the Church of the Holy Sepulcher. He was buried by Joseph of Arimathaea, a secret follower. Three days later, His tomb was found empty, and over the next 40 days His followers joyfully reported His return from death. From that time they dedicated themselves to teaching that Jesus had died and risen again to offer eternal life to all.

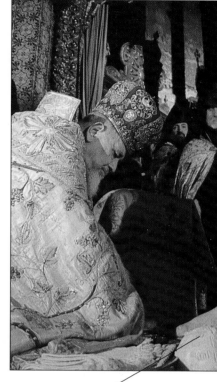

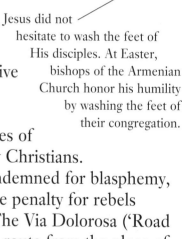

The Chapel of the Ascension marks where Jesus's post-Resurrection ministry ended on the Mount of Olives (*Acts I*). Here, He gave His disciples His final message before He ascended to Heaven.

Jesus did not hesitate to wash the feet of His disciples. At Easter, bishops of the Armenian Church honor his humility by washing the feet of their congregation.

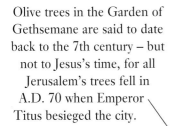

Olive trees in the Garden of Gethsemane are said to date back to the 7th century – but not to Jesus's time, for all Jerusalem's trees fell in A.D. 70 when Emperor Titus besieged the city.

To the Romans, crucifixion was a shameful death for felons. Today, it has become the universal Christian sign that God so loved the world, He gave His only begotten Son to redeem it.

❏ Traditional belief says that Jesus was crucified on a hill. The place of his death is called Golgotha ('Place of the Skull') in the Aramaic tongue, and Calvary in Greek and Latin. However, the Bible nowhere states that the execution took place on a hill.

❏ The Cross (above), the universal Christian symbol, has been an ornamental or sacred motif in many cultures, and exists in many forms. Heraldry recognizes nearly 400 varieties, including the Tau (T-shaped), St Andrew's (X-shaped), Patriarchal (with double crossbar), and Calvary (Christ's) crosses.

❏ Legend tells that Joseph of Arimathaea took Christianity to Britain – with two relics, the Spear of Longinus, which pierced Christ's side, and the Holy Grail, His cup at the Last Supper. Joseph is said to have founded Glastonbury Abbey in Somerset, where his wooden staff took root to become the famous Glastonbury Thorn, which blooms every Christmas to honor Christ's birth.

The four Gospel makers

The Gospels of Matthew, Mark, Luke, and John, which describe Jesus's life and teachings, are generally believed to have been written soon after His death (although some modern scholars dispute this). Matthew and John were eyewitnesses, among Christ's closest companions, the Apostles. Matthew had been a despised tax collector, and John a fisherman, who (though Jesus nicknamed him and his brother James 'sons of thunder' for their hot tempers) is remembered as 'the disciple Jesus loved.' Mark probably, and Luke certainly, never met Jesus, but knew those who had. The first Christians met in the house of Mark's mother, Mary, in Jerusalem, and Mark became St. Paul's (*pages 74-75*) friend and helper. The Apostle Peter called him 'my son Mark,' and is said to have been the source of his Gospel. Luke, a Greek-speaking doctor (traditionally from Antioch, Syria) and the only Gentile of the Gospel-makers, was also a friend of Paul and got his information directly from the Apostles and first Christians. The four Gospels differ in emphasis. Those of Matthew, Mark, and Luke – called the Synoptic ('seeing together') Gospels – speak chiefly of Christ's ministry in Galilee. John describes more of Christ's labors in Judaea, and places more stress on Christ's own testimony that He was the incarnate Son of God. Mark focuses on Jesus's deeds; Matthew on His teachings; Luke on His foundation of Christianity; and John on His divinity. St. Jerome (c.347-420) took the four beasts of the vision in John's Revelation as symbols of the Gospel writers: the man for Matthew; the lion for Mark; the ox for Luke; the eagle for John.

St. John, as portrayed by an 8th-century Celtic monk. He holds a scroll representing his Gospel; the eagle which is his symbol appears at his shoulder.

The symbol of St. Mark is the winged lion, here carved by 12th-century craftsmen over the door of Angers Cathedral, France.

The Sea of Galilee, where Jesus called two fishermen from net-mending to become 'fishers of men' – as Gospel-writer St. John 'the Divine' and his brother, St. James the Greater.

Papias of Hierapolis (c.140) said Mark 'neither heard the Lord nor followed him,' but based his Gospel on what Peter told him. But many believe Mark was the young man present when Christ was arrested in Gethsemane.

A 9th-century miniature depicts St. Matthew as a medieval French scholar, writing his Gospel at a desk with a quill pen. His eyes are turned, not on his work but upward towards his heavenly inspiration.

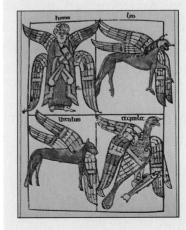
73

Paul: 'Apostle of the Gentiles'

In spite of political and religious opposition, the first Christians made many converts. Preaching the new doctrine to Gentiles (non-Jews) became the special task of St. Paul. Saul, as he was first known, a Jew with Roman citizenship, was born in Tarsus (south Turkey) and studied in Jerusalem to be a rabbi. A strict Pharisee, he was among the leading foes of Christianity, but in c.33, on the way to combat the spread of the new belief in Damascus, he was dramatically converted by a vision of Christ. He preached Christianity at Damascus, but hostility from Jews and understandable mistrust by Christians forced him to spend years in retirement. He re-emerged to help Barnabas establish Christianity in the great city of Antioch, and in c.47, after meeting in Jerusalem with Peter and James, began some 10,000mi (16, 100km) of missionary travels: first to Cyprus and Galatia; then to Greece, from Macedonia south to Athens and Corinth; then to Ephesus (west Turkey), where he spent three years and founded a Christian church. His Epistles (letters) record hazardous journeys by land and sea, threatened by robbers or betrayed by 'false brethren.' Several times only his Roman citizenship saved him from punishment at the hands of orthodox Judaism or pagan cults. In c.58 he returned to Jerusalem to plan a mission through Rome to Spain. But some citizens rioted against him, and he was imprisoned and sent to Rome for trial. He is said to have been martyred there in c.66 at the order of Emperor Nero. His labors as 'Apostle of the Gentiles' ensured the growth of Christianity from a local cult to a world religion.

Many-breasted Diana of Ephesus – not the Roman deity of that name, but an eastern fertility goddess – had a great cult. When Paul won Christian converts in Ephesus, it led to mass riots – headed by the silversmiths who made effigies of the goddess.

Paul's belief that Jesus came to save all peoples, not just the Jews, led him to carry the message of Christianity across much of the known world. This 12th-century enamel portrays Paul preaching to Jews and Greeks.

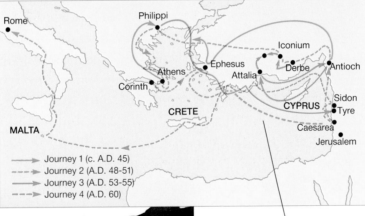

Rome
Philippi
Iconium
Ephesus
Athens
Attalia
Derbe
Antioch
Corinth
CYPRUS
Sidon
Tyre
CRETE
Caesarea
MALTA
Jerusalem

→ Journey 1 (c. A.D. 45)
⇢ Journey 2 (A.D. 48-51)
→ Journey 3 (A.D. 53-55)
⇢ Journey 4 (A.D. 60)

Paul's missionary journeys are described by his friend St. Luke, in the Book of Acts. His own reports appear in his letters to the Christian churches at Corinth, Galatia, Ephesus, Philippi, Colossae, and Thessalonica.

The road to Corinth, where the orthodox Jews accused Paul of blasphemy, but Roman governor Gallio 'cared for none of these things' and refused to pass judgement.

FACT FILE

❑ The term 'Christian' was first used by the Antioch (south Turkey) community established by Barnabas and Paul. Both saints, although not among Jesus's 'Twelve,' are usually styled Apostles.

❑ It is sometimes said that Nero acquitted Paul. He may have returned to Ephesus, and possibly carried out his planned Spanish mission, before being arrested again, brought back to Rome, and beheaded.

❑ A writer of the 2nd century describes Paul as a man of unimpressive appearance – small, bald, and bow-legged. But his influence on the development of Christianity was immense. He did not merely spread the word, but examined and interpreted Christ's teachings.

❑ While Paul's part in spreading Christianity is recorded in the New Testament, the later history of other Apostles is less well documented. St. Andrew is traditionally held to have traveled into Europe, where he is credited with founding the Russian Church. The 'Thomas Christians' of Kerala, India, claim that St. Thomas traveled to India to bring Christianity to their ancestors.

❑ Paul's ban on women singing in church was upheld until the 17th century – and led to the castration of boy sopranos for church choirs.

75

Masada: death on the rock

Masada was not simply a fortress. This synagogue was one of many buildings of a small city built on the rock by order of Herod the Great from around 30 B.C.

Roman rule in Palestine was opposed by Jewish nationalists called Zealots. In A.D. 66, enraged by savage taxation, many moderate Jews joined the Zealots in revolt, seizing Jerusalem's massively fortified Temple complex and strongholds elsewhere. Emperor Nero sent Titus Flavius Vespasianus (9-79) with c.60,000 men to put down the rising. He subdued Galilee, where Jotapata fortress fell after a 47 day siege, and advanced on Jerusalem. He considered peace talks, but when he was recalled to deal with civil war in Italy (and to become Emperor Vespasian in 69), neither his successor, his son Titus (39-81), nor the Zealot leaders was willing to seek peace. Titus besieged Jerusalem, breaching its outer walls after artillery duels between catapults. He starved out the Jews, crucifying captives in sight of those still holding out. At last the Romans stormed the Temple, which they looted and burned. Jewish survivors were sold as slaves, or taken to be exhibited in Titus's triumph at Rome (where he followed his father as Emperor in 79). One fortress still held out: the mountaintop stronghold of Masada, towering c.1,300ft (395m) above the Dead Sea shore and accessible only by the secret 'Snake Path.' Fewer than 1,000 men, women, and children under Elazar ben Yair held Masada for nearly two years against some 15,000 men of the Tenth Legion. Using Jewish slave labor, the Romans built a huge earth ramp to the summit, brought up siege towers and battering rams, and breached the wall. They entered the fortress to find only two women and five children alive: the rest had committed suicide. In Israel today, army recruits climb to the fortress to swear 'Masada will not fall again.'

Titus's capture of Jerusalem was celebrated with a triumphal parade in which Jewish holy objects looted from the Temple, like the seven-branched menorah, were shown.

At the northern end of the mighty rock of Masada Herod built his 'hanging palace,' a luxurious place of refuge extending down three terraces.

The remains of the huge earthwork siege ramp constructed by the Romans to storm Masada can be seen leading up to the rock's main fortress.

❏ Joseph ben Mathias (c.37-95), defeated commander at Jotapata fortress, changed sides after his capture and, as a honored citizen at Rome, where he was called Flavius Josephus, became a famous historian. His *Bellum Judaicum* ('Jewish War') provides an eyewitness history of the revolt; he wrote also a history of the Jewish people from the Creation to his own time. Many Jewish scholars maintain that Josephus was a traitor who deliberately sold the fortress to win Roman favor.

❏ The typical ballista (catapult) used by both Romans and Jews at the siege of Jerusalem could throw a 55lb (25kg) rock to a range of c.220-440yd (200-400m). Propulsion was provided by twisted sinews (animal tendons) or ropes: the longest-ranged ballistae were said to be those whose torsion ropes were made of women's hair. They also had 'scorpions' (tripod mounted crossbows), anti-personnel weapons firing armor piercing metal bolts of up to 7.5lb (3.5kg) weight.

❏ Jewish legend says that Titus made worse his sacrilege in destroying the Temple by conducting a love affair with Berenice, sister of Herod Agrippa II, the Romanized Jew whom the Romans made a puppet ruler in Judaea in 70. God punished Titus by having a bluebottle fly lay eggs in his ear: they hatched, and the incessant buzzing in his head caused fits of madness.

Diaspora: the Jews' long exile

Some date the Jewish Diaspora (Greek: dispersal) from the destruction of the Temple by Titus in A.D. 70 (*pages 76-77*). But for some centuries before that time more Jews had lived outside Judaea than in it. In Jewish reckoning, the Temple's fall and the Second Revolt (132-135) mark the beginning of the *Galuth* (Hebrew: exile): more than 1,800 years during which the Jews were stateless people. Emperor Hadrian, tired of the Jews' constant opposition to Rome, announced in c.132 that he would rebuild Jerusalem as a non-Jewish city and settle pagan colonists in Judaea. He ordered a temple to Jupiter erected on the Temple site, and forbade Jewish religious rites. The Jews rose under Simon bar-Kochba, whom Rabbi Akiba, most respected teacher of the time, hailed as Messiah. The rising had been well prepared; bar-Kochba won several victories and drove the Romans out of Judaea. But Hadrian poured in men, up to eight of his finest legions, and brought his best general, Julius Severus, from Britain to take command. After nearly three years' war, bar-Kochba was besieged in his last stronghold, Bethar near Jerusalem, where he died fighting. Hadrian took savage reprisals. Akiba and other rabbis were tortured to death (one roasted on a fire made of *Torah* scrolls); their followers were massacred or sold into slavery; all Jews were driven from Jerusalem (renamed Aelia Capitolina) and from much of Judaea (renamed Syria Palaestina). Deprived of their holy heartland, they began the centuries of exile that would not end until the raising of the Star of David flag signalled the birth of the State of Israel in 1948.

Ahasuerus, the 'Wandering Jew' of medieval legend, doomed to walk the earth until Christ's second coming, is seen here in an early 19th century book illustration.

This sandal from the 'Cave of Letters' at Nahal Hever, near the shore of the Dead Sea, probably shod one of bar-Kochba's rebels.

Survivors of bar-Kochba's rising hid in caves in the Judaean desert, where artefacts like this basket were found in a near perfect state of preservation

A container of woven osiers (willow rods) found at Nahal Hever.

The caves formed underground villages: perhaps these were the keys to a storehouse or armory.

The cave dwellers ate with spoons from well turned wooden plates – until their stores ran out.

This mirror and jewel box (above right) belonged to the wife of a Jewish fighting man.

This letter sent by bar-Kochba to one of his men was found in a Dead Sea cave at Wadi Murabba'at. Like the correspondence in the 'Cave of Letters,' it was preserved for nearly two thousand years by the dry heat of the desert.

FACT FILE

❏ The name of Simon bar-Kochba ('Son of a Star') signified his claim to be Messiah. It was taken from the Book of Numbers (Chapter 24; Verse 17): ' . . . there shall come a Star out of Jacob, and a Sceptre shall rise out of Israel . . . and destroy all the children of Sheth.' He was supremely confident of victory, praying in public: 'Lord, do not help the enemy; but as for us, we need no help.'

❏ Much of what we know of bar-Kochba's rising comes from recently uncovered Dead Sea caves, fortified as refuges by his followers. The 'Cave of Letters' yielded coins struck at his command, dated in the years of 'the freedom of Israel,' and his personal letters. The 'Cave of Horrors' contained the skeletons of 40 men, women, and children who had starved to death when trapped by the Romans.

❏ For centuries after Hadrian's time, Jews were allowed into Jerusalem on only one day in the year, the anniversary of the Temple's destruction, when they were allowed to pray at its site – at the so-called 'Wailing Wall (above).'

Martyrs for the faith

At first Rome neither actively persecuted Christians, nor protected them from attacks by Jewish or pagan leaders. Roman provincial governors were mainly concerned to keep good order in their territories: so long as taxes were paid, they did not interfere unduly with their subjects' internal affairs. But as Christians grew in number, their refusal to worship Roman gods – especially their refusal to revere the god-emperor – was increasingly seen as an expression of political opposition to Roman rule. When fire destroyed half of Rome in 64, Emperor Nero made the unpopular Christians the scapegoats, and began an intensive drive against them. Thousands of Christians died in prison from ill treatment, were crucified, burned, or killed by wild beasts in the arenas: 'butchered to make a Roman holiday.' Survivors met in secret. They literally went underground, taking refuge in the catacombs, Rome's subterranean cemeteries, whose walls still bear Christian graffiti: the Cross, the fish, the Greek letters XP (for 'Christos'). After Nero's death, the Church enjoyed a short remission from active persecution, but under later rulers such as Domitian (ruled 81-96) they were once again executed or exiled for refusing to follow the state religion, not only in Rome but throughout the Empire. Persecution continued to a greater or lesser degree until the reign (306-337) of Constantine. The steadfastness with which Christian martyrs kept to their faith, and the courage with which they faced death, served to win more to their cause. Attacked on all sides, by Romans, Jews, and pagan peoples, Christianity nevertheless continued to spread.

St. Lucy was an early martyr at Syracuse. Her history is lost: legend says she was miraculously preserved when drawn by oxen, exposed in a brothel, and cast into fire: her frustrated executioners finally stabbed her.

Catacombs were Christian meeting places as well as tombs. Walls were painted with religious themes – here, Christ breaks bread with His Apostles.

Emperor Nero ordered the trial and execution of thousands of Christians – on the charge of 'hatred of the human race.'

Rome's early Christians cut underground cemeteries: long tunnels, where the dead lay on shelves cut in the rock walls. Later these tunnels, or catacombs, proved refuges from persecution.

❏ The first Christians met in their own homes for the 'breaking of bread' together, in memory of Christ's Last Supper. In time the breaking of bread ceased to be part of an actual meal and became the ceremony of the Eucharist (Lord's Supper, Holy Communion, or Mass).

❏ An early Christian rite blending worship and charity was the *agape* ('love feast'), where the rich feasted the poor. Pagan writers played on its name to suggest the *agape* was a drunken, sexual orgy. In some cases there was truth in the allegations, and in 397 the Church forbade the old rite.

❏ The Greek word *ichthus*, 'fish', is made up of the initial letters of the words 'Jesus Christ, Son of God, Savior.' Christians adopted the symbol of the fish as a secret sign to identify themselves.

❏ Entire Christian congregations died together rather than betray their faith. In 177, the members of the churches of Lyons and Vienne (modern France) were accused of such crimes as cannibalism and incest, tortured, and executed. The 48 'Martyrs of Lyons' ranged from from 90-year-old Bishop Pothinus, who died from a savage beating, to the slave girl Blandina, gored to death by a wild bull in the arena. The martyrs were even denied burial: their broken bodies were thrown into the Rhône River.

The company of saints

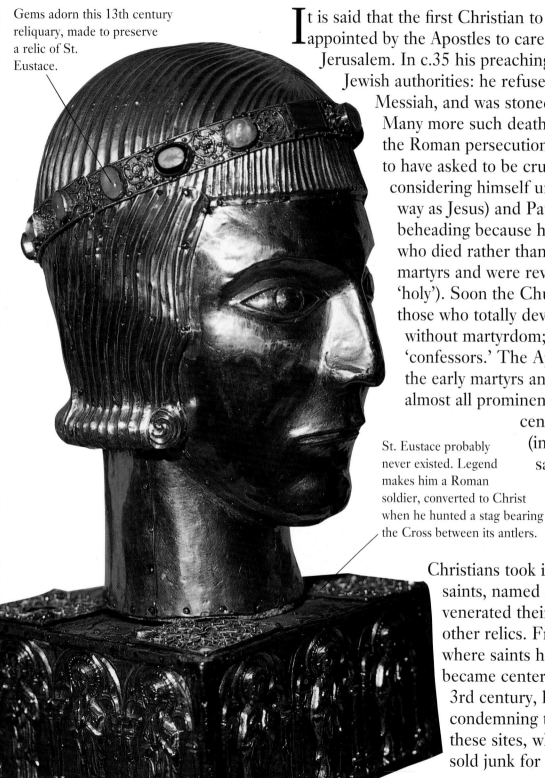

Gems adorn this 13th century reliquary, made to preserve a relic of St. Eustace.

It is said that the first Christian to die for the faith was Stephen, appointed by the Apostles to care for Christian widows in Jerusalem. In c.35 his preaching brought him before the Jewish authorities: he refused to deny that Jesus was Messiah, and was stoned to death for blasphemy. Many more such deaths followed. Those who died in the Roman persecutions included Peter (who is said to have asked to be crucified upside down, considering himself unworthy to suffer in the same way as Jesus) and Paul, given the 'dignity' of beheading because he was a Roman citizen. Those who died rather than betray their faith were called martyrs and were revered as saints (Latin: *sanctus*, 'holy'). Soon the Church also regarded as saints those who totally devoted their lives to God, even without martyrdom; these saints are called 'confessors.' The Apostles, the Virgin Mary, and the early martyrs and confessors (in practice, almost all prominent churchmen of the 1st-8th centuries) received canonization (inclusion in the canon, list, of saints) by general consent.

St. Eustace probably never existed. Legend makes him a Roman soldier, converted to Christ when he hunted a stag bearing the Cross between its antlers.

From about the 10th century saints had to be established through a formal process, still in use today.

Christians took inspiration from the lives of saints, named children in their honor, and venerated their tombs, bodily remains, and other relics. From earliest times, places where saints had lived, died, or were buried became centers of pilgrimage. As early as the 3rd century, leading churchmen were condemning the 'commercialization' of these sites, where peddlers of phoney relics sold junk for huge sums.

Splendid reliquaries attest how kings and churches thought money well spent in obtaining and housing holy relics.

St. Peter's martyrdom at Rome under Nero is history, his crucifixion upside-down probably legend. The altar of the Vatican basilica is said to mark his tomb.

The Eastern and Western churches often fail to agree upon canonization, but St Ignatius (painted here by Rubens) is one of those recognized by both.

FACT FILE

❏ Among the early saints were holy hermits, who fled the world to devote themselves to prayer. St. Simeon Stylites (above) (c.390-459) took this to extremes. 'Despairing of escaping the world horizontally, he tried to escape it vertically' – and for the last 36 years of his life lived, prayed, and preached from the top of a 65ft (20m) pillar.

❏ Of more than 4,500 saints known today, many of the earliest are recognized by the Church to be legendary – including England's patron, St. George, and the traveler's protector St. Christopher.

❏ The modern process of canonization may take centuries. Joan of Arc (d.1431) was not made a saint until 1920. She was canonized for her 'exemplary life:' before her execution she had been condemned by the Church for witchcraft and heresy, so she could not be regarded legitimately as a martyr.

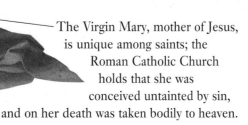

The Virgin Mary, mother of Jesus, is unique among saints; the Roman Catholic Church holds that she was conceived untainted by sin, and on her death was taken bodily to heaven.

'In this sign, conquer'

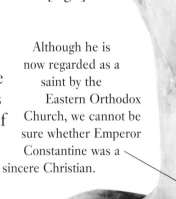

If one thing was needed to assure the triumph of the Christian faith over paganism, it was the adoption of Christianity as 'official' faith of the Roman Empire. Emperor Constantine I the Great (c.274-337) did not 'convert' the Empire to Christianity. He himself was first a Sun-worshiper, and was not baptised a Christian – and then by a 'heretical' Arian (*pages 94-95*) bishop – until shortly before his death. His sympathy for Christianity was perhaps based partly on genuine religious feeling, partly on political considerations. Son of Western Emperor Constantius I (there had been separate Western and Eastern rulers since 293), he was hailed Emperor by his legions in Britain on his father's death at Eboracum (York) in 306. Until 312 he ruled only Britain and Gaul, but in that year he defeated a rival claimant, Maxentius, at the battle of Milvian Bridge, near Rome. He credited his victory to a pre-battle vision of Christ's Cross, seen against the Sun, with the words '*In hoc vinces*' ('In this [sign] conquer'). In 313, as master of the West, he ordered at Milan that Christianity should be 'tolerated' throughout the Empire. With the threat of persecution removed, the spread of the faith rapidly increased – and to some extent this was, as Constantine no doubt hoped, a source of political stability. By 323 Constantine was strong enough to overthrow Licinius, Emperor of the East, and once more unite the Empire. Christianity was then strongest in the Eastern (Greek speaking) provinces, and among Constantine's first acts was to establish his new capital in the East at Constantinople (old Byzantium).

A formal bust of Flavius Valerius Aurelius Constantinus who, as Emperor Constantine I, was the sole ruler of the Roman Empire in 324-337.

Although he is now regarded as a saint by the Eastern Orthodox Church, we cannot be sure whether Emperor Constantine was a sincere Christian.

Constantine's change of capital was to enable the Roman Empire to survive when Rome fell in 476.

The massive Arch of Constantine, near the Colosseum in Rome, was built in 315 to mark the Emperor's victory at the Milvian Bridge.

The decorations of the Arch reflect the Emperor's military and political triumphs rather than his religious beliefs.

A wall painting of the early Christian era shows Constantine, inspired by his vision of the Cross, defeating his rival for the imperial throne, Maxentius, at the Milvian Bridge in 312.

Julian, last of the pagans

King Shapur I initiated Persia's power struggle against Rome, continued by his son Narses and won by his grandson Shapur II – in the course of which Julian fell.

Constantine the Great made Christianity the recognized religion of the Roman Empire. Some 25 years after his death his nephew made a determined attempt to restore paganism. Flavius Claudius Julian(us) (332-363) spent his early life as a student of philosophy at Athens. In 355, as the only other surviving male of Constantine's family, he was made commander in the West by his cousin Emperor Constantius II. Julian, the unknown scholar, proved a fine general. Campaigning in Gaul, he decisively defeated the Germanic King Chnodomar at Argentoratum (Strasbourg) in 357, personally rallying his *clibanarii* (heavy cavalry, with both rider and horse protected by body armor) after they had fled a German attack.

Julian was brought up in the Christian faith, but rejected it after studying eastern philosophies.

Constantius, now jealous, tried to take over his best legions. But Julian's troops refused to leave their leader, and instead proclaimed him Emperor; civil war was averted by Constantius's death in 361. Julian believed that Rome's strength had been weakened by Christianity, and announced he would restore the old, pagan religion. Privileges granted to Christian clergy and teachers were canceled; money grants to churches redirected to the restoration of pagan temples and revival of old rites. Christians later called Julian the 'Apostate' ('treacherous rebel'), but in fact his policy had little effect: there was no outright persecution of Christians – and most people were just not interested in his ideas. His reign was too short (c.18 months) for his reforms to take effect. In 363, campaigning against Shapur II of Persia, he was killed in action. In 392, Emperor Theodosius forbade worship of pagan gods throughout the Empire.

In his theological writings, Julian condemned Christianity as not merely false but atheistical.

Julian wanted to revive the mystery cult of the god Mithras, chief rival to Christianity, with which it had elements in common.

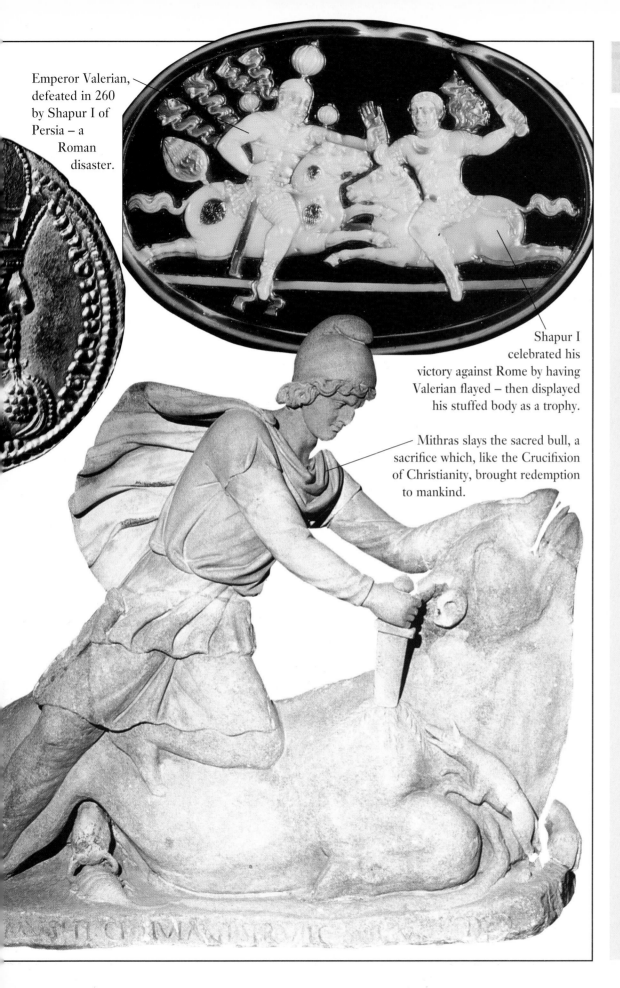

Emperor Valerian, defeated in 260 by Shapur I of Persia – a Roman disaster.

Shapur I celebrated his victory against Rome by having Valerian flayed – then displayed his stuffed body as a trophy.

Mithras slays the sacred bull, a sacrifice which, like the Crucifixion of Christianity, brought redemption to mankind.

❏ Many people mocked Julian for his enthusiasm for old customs. He was satirized for wearing a beard – traditional mark of an Athenian philosopher – which in Julian's time was regarded as showing a hopeless lack of 'street cred.' Julian himself wrote a satire against his attackers, and titled it *Misopogon* ('Beard Hater').

❏ Traditionally, Julian's dying words were '*Vicisti, Galilaee*' ('Thou hast conquered, O Galilean'). Perhaps these words were put into his mouth by Christian writers anxious to stress that the 'Apostate' had been struck down by the power of Jesus. Some pagan writers, however, claimed that they proved he had been stabbed in the back by a Christian secret agent among his bodyguard.

❏ The Greek philosophy that inspired Julian's paganism was thereafter hated and feared by many Christians. In 415 the philosopher and mathematician Hypatia was tortured to death by a Christian mob – allegedly directed by the Bishop, St. Cyril – at Alexandria. Hypatia was resented and distrusted by the 'Church fathers' because, as well as being a leading Greek scholar of the time, she was a woman.

❏ When Constantine the Great died, his successor Constantius slew all possible claimants to the throne. Only five year old Julian was spared.

The power of the papacy

Not all Popes have been good men, but historians agree on the holiness of St. Gregory the Great (540-604). Legend says that Christ Himself appeared to bless Gregory's Mass.

The early Christian churches made decisions on doctrine and forms of worship by democratic (if sometimes heated) discussion. No one church had authority over others. But as rival schools of Christian thought emerged, a central authority was needed to prevent the fragmentation of the Church. This role was to be taken by the Church of Rome, with a claim to authority based on 'apostolic succession.' This holds that the authority of all bishops comes from Christ through the Apostles: the Bishop of Rome, as successor to Peter, the Apostles' leader, is thus the prime authority. In the year 96 Pope Clement I first exerted Rome's supremacy, by intervening to settle a dispute between the Bishop of Corinth and his congregation. Clement is counted as the third Pope, after Peter and Linus, but the title (*papa*, 'father') was then used by all bishops. It was not reserved for the Bishop of Rome until 1073. It was inevitable that the center of Christianity should be in Rome, then the world's center of power; but this led from very early times to charges that the Church's leaders were 'playing politics,' and favoring the rich and powerful. Pope Callistus (Calixtus) I (in office 218-222) was accused of allowing wealthy sinners to buy forgiveness. Papal power grew fast after Emperor Constantine's decree of toleration for Christianity in 313. Pope Leo I the Great's (c.390-461) active role in both religious and political affairs – he was credited with persuading Attila the Hun to turn away from his attack on Rome – firmly established the authority of the papacy.

An ancient painting shows the basilica (cathedral) erected by Emperor Constantine to honor the Apostle Peter, regarded by the Roman Church as the first Pope.

Castel Sant'Angelo, Rome, was built as a tomb by Emperor Hadrian in A.D. 139. It later became a fortress where Popes took refuge when their authority was challenged.

Constantinople, source of this ring with Christian symbols, was Rome's religious rival.

❑ For centuries every Pope has used the 'Fisherman's Ring,' a signet showing St. Peter fishing from a boat, to seal official documents. When a Pope dies his ring is destroyed and a new one made for his successor.

❑ In 258 Pope Sixtus II and six of his deacons were martyred. A surviving deacon, Lawrence, was ordered to hand over the church's wealth. He produced a crowd of poor folk, saying 'Here is the church's treasure.' He was probably beheaded, but legend says he was roasted on a grid – mocking his executioners: 'Why don't you turn me over: this side is already cooked.'

❑ Traditionally a Pope adopts a new name on taking office. Sergius II (in office 844-847) is said to have been the first to do so, but sources disagree on both his original name and his motive. Some say he was called 'Hogsmouth' – good reason for change. Others say his real name was Peter, but he judged himself unworthy to bear the same name as the Apostle. John, used by 23 Popes (including 2 medieval 'anti-popes'), has been the name most frequently adopted.

❑ A Pope is also called Supreme Pontiff, and Vicar of Christ (a title taken by Innocent III in 1198). A more humble name, used by Gregory the Great (590-604), is *Servus Servorum Dei* ('Servant of the Servants of God').

A light for the Gentiles

The Roman Empire at first tried to crush Christianity, but Roman civilization in fact aided the spread of the new faith. Its excellent roads and sea lanes meant that the word of Jesus was quickly carried to new outposts, and that the early churches could keep in contact. Jerusalem, fount of Christianity, was soon a less important center than Rome, Antioch, Ephesus, and Alexandria. By the 2nd century there were more Christian communities outside Palestine than within it. Christianity had become a mainly Gentile religion. As it spread, it acquired doctrines much more complex than the teachings of Jesus. The Church of Alexandria – said to have been founded by St. Mark – was particularly influential. Its teachers helped shape Christian belief by uniting Jesus's words with Greek philosophy. Some of its members left their homes and worldly goods to devote themselves to prayer, alone or in small groups, thus beginning the monastic movement. The churches of Asia Minor produced great teachers like St. Polycarp, Bishop of Smyrna, martyred at the age of 86 in c.155. From the church at the Roman trade center of Carthage (Tunisia), the faith spread through North Africa. From churches within the Roman Empire, missionaries carried the word at first to the East, into Persia and India, then to the 'barbarian' peoples of Western Europe. By the 2nd century, Lyons, France, was an important Christian community, where St. Irenaeus (c.130-202), a disciple of St. Polycarp from Smyrna, became one of the most important teachers of the period. By 300, Britain too had a number of Christian communities, notably at London, York, and Colchester.

The Gallarus Oratory, a small boat-shaped stone church, defies dating but may be Ireland's oldest surviving church. Christianity reached Ireland by the 5th century, traditionally via St. Patrick.

The long-lost Ark of the Covenant is said to have come to rest here, at the ancient Cathedral of St. Mary of Zion, Axum, North Ethiopia.

The Roman province of Cappadocia (modern Turkey) was a major Christian center from the 1st century. These rock dwellings housed medieval Christians.

A missionary Bible: the Gothic translation, copied c.500.

When 4th-century bishop Ulfilas translated the Gospel for the Goths, he had to expand both their alphabet and language to express ideas wholly new to them.

FACT FILE

❑ The 'desert fathers' who began the monastic movement sought God through solitude and simple living. Some took self-denial to extremes, starving, whipping, or castrating themselves; even engaging in contests to see who could undergo the most 'holy discomfort.' The Egyptian hermit St. Anthony (b. (c.251), often considered the true founder of monasticism, disapproved such excesses. He mastered the temptations of the flesh by prayer, and is consequently said to have lived in perfect health to the age of more than 100.

❑ Legend has it that Christianity was brought to France in the 1st century by St. Amadour, servant of the Virgin Mary and husband of St. Veronica. He is credited with founding the Shrine of Our Lady at Rocamadour, southwest France. France's patron, St. Denis, is now generally believed to be a composite figure, reflecting missionaries of the 2nd-3rd centuries.

❑ Tradition says that Britain acquired its first Christian martyr in c.209, when St. Alban of Verulamium (modern St. Albans) was beheaded during the persecutions ordered by Emperor Diocletian. His death is said to have been attended by miracles, which converted many spectators. The Abbey of St. Albans commemorates his martyrdom, but modern scholars doubt it happened.

The word of God

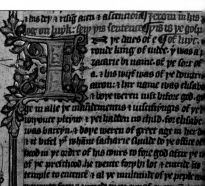
The Old Testament (*Septuagint*) was translated into Greek by Jewish scholars in the 3rd century B.C.; the New Testament was written in Greek. In c.384, Pope Damasus commissioned the great scholar St. Jerome to produce the Latin *Vulgate* (Common Version), still standard in the Roman Catholic Church. Other early Bibles still in use include the *Peshitta*, a 4th century translation into Syriac (Aramaic dialect); and a 3rd century Coptic (Egyptian) version. English Bibles first appeared in the 700s with Anglo-Saxon versions (now lost) by Aldhelm and Bede. Medieval churchmen, fearing 'common people' would misinterpret the Book, opposed such translations as John Wycliffe's English Vulgate (1384). Printing made Bibles far more widely available: the first printed Bible was Johann Gutenberg's Latin edition of 1456. Erasmus's Greek New Testament of 1516 paid more scholarly attention to early texts, as did Martin Luther's German Bible. In England, churchmen still opposed translations like William Tyndale's New Testament (1526) and Myles Coverdale's Bible (1535), but in 1538 all English churches were ordered to make a translation available to parishioners. This produced the *Great Bible* of 1538, the *Geneva Bible* of 1560, the Bishops' Bible of 1568 – and the King James' Bible (*Authorized Version*) of 1611, the definitive English Bible for some 350 years. A *Revised Version*, based on an older Greek text, appeared in 1881. In the present century, versions based on new research into ancient texts and written in modern language include the *New English Bible* (1946), *Jerusalem Bible* (1966), and *Good News Bible* (1976).

Before printing, hand-copied Bibles were illuminated – literally 'lit up' with glowing pictures, patterns, and decorated letters.

Copyists usually opened each Gospel with a full-page picture of the appropriate Evangelist. Here a bearded St. Luke is portrayed writing his Gospel.

St. Jerome's translation of the Psalms. For the Gospels, Jerome revised existing Latin versions: the Psalms were his own translation from Greek and Hebrew.

The 15th century artist has provided the saint with the luxury of a revolving bookstand to hold his texts.

St. Jerome, at work on his translation of the Bible. The cardinal's hat hanging behind him symbolizes his services as Pope Damasus's secretary.

Jerome's 'pen and paper' were quills (feathers) and parchment (hides, smoothed with pumice stone) or, for best, vellum (fine skins of very young animals).

❏ The *Septuagint* (from Latin *septuaginta*, 'seventy') is so called because it is said to be the work of 72 scholars, who toiled for 72 days at the great library of Alexandria.

❏ Early missionaries sometimes had to invent an alphabet before they could translate the Bible for converts. St. Mesrop (c.345-439) did so for the Armenians: his New Testament is still standard in the Armenian Church. St. Cyril (c.827-869) created the Cyrillic alphabet for Slavonic tribes; today his Bible remains the official version of the Russian Orthodox Church.

❏ The 'Wicked Bible' of 1631 omitted the word 'not' from the seventh commandment, making it 'Thou shalt commit adultery.' Its publisher was heavily fined. Some editions are nicknamed for odd translations. The 'Bug Bible' of 1535 gives 'bugs' instead of 'terrors' – 'Thou shalt not nede to be afrayed for eny bugges by night.' The 'Treacle Bible' of 1568 uses 'treacle' for 'balm' – 'Is there no tryacle in Gilead?' In 1971, the 'Bathroom Bible' updated a Hebrew euphemism thus: 'Saul went into a cave to go to the bathroom.'

❏ The Bible has been translated in full into 318 languages, and partially into 1,628 languages and dialects. The *Good News Bible* in English is estimated to have sold more than 111,000,000 copies in 1976-91.

Battles over belief

Early Christianity produced many scholars well read in both Judaic and pagan philosophies. Such teachers as St. Augustine (354-430), Bishop of Hippo in North Africa, and St. John Chrysostom (c.347-407), whose name means 'Golden Mouth' or 'the Eloquent,' Archbishop of Constantinople, produced learned commentaries on the Gospels. Their contributions to Christian thought have had immense influence to the present day. But, unhappily, the work of many fine scholars also served to change the simple teachings of Jesus into a morass of complex doctrines and speculations. A major task of the early Church was to establish a single, 'official' standard of belief. Teachings that were unacceptable to the most powerful Church leaders came to be condemned as heresies. The application of Greek philosophy to Christian thought by the great doctrinal writers of the school of Alexandria – including Clement (c.150-215) and Origen (185-254) – contributed to the Gnostic heresy, which was alleged to value Greek and Oriental texts equally with the Gospels. The Alexandrian priest Arius (c.250-336) denied Christ's divinity, arguing that Jesus was God's creation and not His equal. The British monk Pelagius (c.350-420) denied the existence of original sin (the idea that Adam's fall contaminated all mankind) and suggested that leading a good life was as important to achieving salvation as God's grace. Gnostics, Arians, and Pelagians were all condemned as heretics at the great Church councils – notably Nicaea (325), Constantinople (381), Ephesus (431), and Chalcedon (451) – called to agree on official doctrine.

Christmas celebrated by the Greek Orthodox Church. The Eastern Orthodox churches remain nearest of all modern Christianity's branches to the forms of the early Church.

St. Augustine created a monastic Rule for his followers. In the 11th century this became the guideline of the Augustinian Canons.

The Church split in the 16th century. Protestant churches rejected the authority of the Pope, regarded by the Roman Catholic Church as the successor of St. Peter.

St. Augustine's works were many as well as scholarly: 113 books and treatises, some 500 sermons, and many letters survive.

❏ The Nicene Creed, still used by the Roman Catholic and Anglican Churches, was formulated by the Council of Nicaea to uphold the Godhead of Christ – 'only-begotten Son of God' – against the Arian heresy. Its central affirmation of 'one, holy, catholic and apostolic church' forbade its followers to credit schools of thought not approved by Church leaders.

❏ An account of the Council of Nicaea says that the Bishop of Myra was so angered by Arius's attempts to defend himself that he punched the heretic on the jaw. The battling bishop has become one of the world's best known and most popular saints – not because of his brawling, but because he is St. Nicholas, the original 'Santa Claus.'

❏ As a young man, St. Augustine was the despair of his pious mother, and only gradually came to accept his call to the Church. In his *Confessions*, recording his reluctant conversion from a worldly life, he tells of his early prayer: 'Lord, make me chaste [pure]; but not yet!'

❏ 'Heresy' means 'chosen things' – referring to the heretic's choice of his own opinion over Church doctrine. In 1233, the Church's drive against heresy led to the horrors of the Inquisition, when anyone thought to hold heretical beliefs was 'put to the question' – tortured.

The Church divided

Disputes over doctrine have long troubled Christianity, leading to charges of heresy (*pages 94-95*), schisms (divisions), and savage and bloody wars. In 451, when Pope Leo the Great of Rome claimed to be supreme head of the Church, the Council of Chalcedon decided that Rome and Constantinople should share authority. But over the years the rift between the Roman (Latin) Church in the West and the Orthodox (Greek) Church of the Byzantine Empire in the East widened. In 1054 the Pope of Rome and Patriarch of Constantinople mutually denounced each other, and the schism became final. Brief attempts at reunion in 1274 and 1439 failed, and not until the 1980s-90s were new attempts to heal the division begun. The Western Church was afflicted by a further 'Great Schism' in 1378. In an attempt to escape political manipulation by Italian noblemen, Pope Clement V moved the papal seat in 1309 from Rome to Avignon in France. The Avignon papacy became just as much a French political pawn as the Roman papacy was an Italian one. In 1378 rival popes elected in Rome and Avignon denounced each other as 'anti-Popes.' The dispute was settled in Rome's favor in 1417, but papal authority had been much weakened. Demands for reform of the Church swelled, and in 1517 the reformers found a great leader, when the German churchman Martin Luther (1483-1546) nailed his '95 Theses,' condemning corrupt practices and errors of faith, to the door of Wittenberg Castle Church. The protest movement of Luther and others, called 'Protestants' from c.1529, demanding 'Reformation' of the Church, ended in the greatest of all Christian schisms: the division between the Roman Catholic and Reformed (Protestant) churches.

A striking portrait by his friend and contemporary Lucas Cranach the Elder (1472-1553) well captures the blend of sincerity and obstinacy in the character of Martin Luther, leader of the Reformation, greatest of all Christian divisions.

The Western and Eastern (Orthodox) Churches separated in 1054. Orthodox belief soon spread to Russia, source of this lovely 15th century icon (religious image).

After the Reformation savage religious wars racked Europe for many years. Catholics and Protestants tortured and killed each other in the name of Christ.

King Henry VIII of England (ruled 1509-47) quarreled with the Pope, who refused to declare void the first of his six marriages. Henry remained a Catholic, but his denial of papal authority prepared the way for the English Reformation.

Pilgrims to the Holy Land

For many centuries Christians have revered as holy places the sites in Palestine, especially in Jerusalem, associated with Jesus's life, death, and resurrection. Pilgrimages from Western Europe to the Holy Land became big business in the Middle Ages, when the act of making the long and dangerous journey to Palestine, through territory held by warlike Muslim peoples, was believed to ensure salvation. The fact that Jerusalem is not a Christian preserve, but a Holy City for Jews and Muslims as well, has caused savage disputes down the ages. The medieval wars called Crusades (11-14th centuries) had their origin in quarrels between Christian and Muslim pilgrims to Jerusalem, where the magnificent Muslim shrine called the Dome of the Rock traditionally marks the place where the Prophet Muhammad was taken up to Heaven. Even within Christianity, the Holy City has aroused unholy quarrels: the Crimean War of 1853-56 originated in a dispute between Orthodox Christians and Roman Catholics over rights to guardianship of the holy places. Today, Christians still make pilgrimages to the Holy Land to visit the Church of the Nativity at Bethlehem, and Golgotha and the Holy Sepulcher in Jerusalem. Different Christian denominations still vie for custodianship of the holy places. At Jerusalem's Church of the Holy Sepulcher, the Greek Orthodox, Roman Catholic, Armenian, Coptic, Ethiopian, and Syrian Churches have evolved a 'time-share' scheme. Other holy sites are shared less peacefully: in 1986, a disagreement over cleaning rights in Bethlehem's Church of the Nativity brought Greek and Armenian clergy to blows.

Built in 687, the gilded dome fell 400 years later and has been restored.

Beneath Jerusalem's great Moslem shrine of the Dome of the Rock lies a stone which Moslems and Jews alike revere as the world's foundation-stone, lying over the primeval waters and the yawning gap of Chaos.

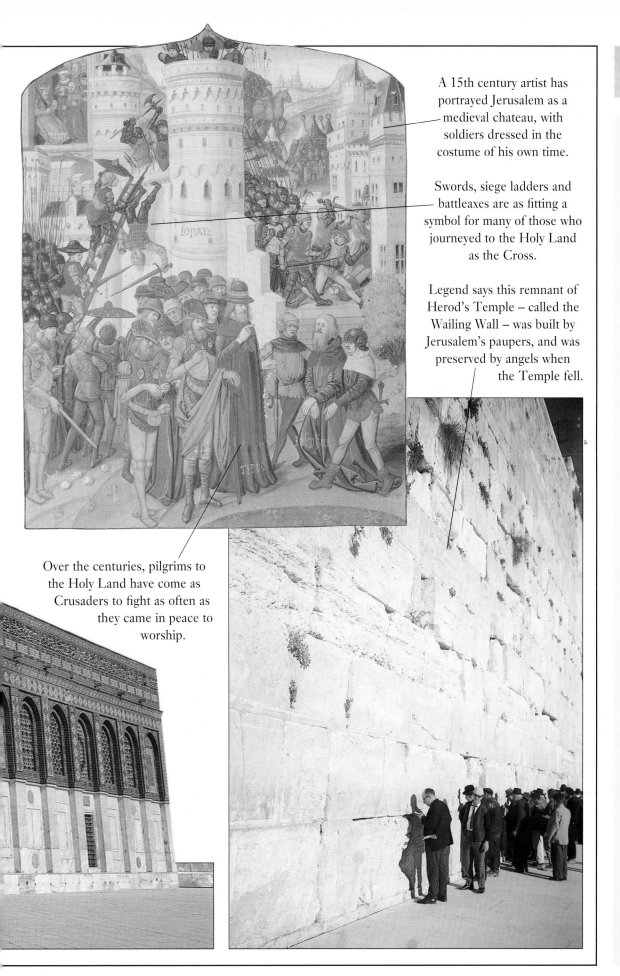

A 15th century artist has portrayed Jerusalem as a medieval chateau, with soldiers dressed in the costume of his own time.

Swords, siege ladders and battleaxes are as fitting a symbol for many of those who journeyed to the Holy Land as the Cross.

Legend says this remnant of Herod's Temple – called the Wailing Wall – was built by Jerusalem's paupers, and was preserved by angels when the Temple fell.

Over the centuries, pilgrims to the Holy Land have come as Crusaders to fight as often as they came in peace to worship.

Pilgrims to the tomb of Jesus have a choice of two: the traditional site of the Holy Sepulcher, and the Garden Tomb (above). Late last century, excavations revealed this rock-cut tomb in the remains of a garden – just as the Gospels describe Jesus's burial place. Although never officially identified as His tomb, it is reverently maintained.

❑ Above the Jewish shrine of King David's Tomb, on Jerusalem's Mount Zion, Crusaders built a Christian shrine, the Cenacle, or Room of the Last Supper, on the supposed site of the 'Upper Room' where Jesus celebrated His last Passover meal with His Disciples. The fact that 13 persons were present at this meal is said to have given rise to the widespread belief that 13 is an unlucky number.

❑ A lesser known pilgrimage site in Palestine is the Galilean tomb said to be that of Jethro, father-in-law of Moses. It is a focus for the worship of the Druzes of Israel, an Arab people whose religious belief (which they traditionally keep secret from non-Druzes) incorporates both Muslim and Judaic elements.

SUPERFACTS

Ancient world
The Hebrews, like other Mesopotamian peoples, held that the world lay between the divided waters of the primeval Ocean. Mountain pillars held the Earth above the Great Deep. Over the Earth arched the solid dome of the heavens; above that lay the waters of the firmament, supplying rain through the 'windows of heaven.'

'Bull and reed' music
Music was one of humanity's earliest inventions. In c.3500 B.C. the popular music of Mesopotamia was 'bull and reed' music: booming drums were the 'bull;' pipes carrying the melody were the 'reed' part.

Sumerian machinery
By c.3500 B.C., Sumerian farmers were drawing up water for their fields with mechanisms known as *dalu*. Today, farmers in lower Iraq still use the same means – the world's oldest machinery.

A long drink
The Sumerians enjoyed their beer. A spectacular find at Ur was a gold drinking tube some 3.5ft (1m) long – a giant 'straw' used to drink from beer jars made on a similar scale.

Queen's burial
Queen Shubad of Ur was buried in c.2600 B.C., in a cloak of gold, silver beads and gemstones, and a rich headdress of gold and lapis lazuli. Her magnificent grave goods included a decorated wooden sledge, with two oxen to draw it; a harp inlaid with shells and colored stones; an inlaid gaming board; and vessels of gold, silver, copper, and pottery. She took her servants with her to death: two female attendants, ten finely dressed court ladies, a harpist, two grooms, and five armed guards.

Protection and punishment ▼
The laws of Hammurabi, ruler of Babylon, were carved on stone pillars. Only one survives (below): its 3,600 lines explain 282 laws, with 16 lines blessing the law-abiding – and 280 lines cursing the disobedient. The laws protected the weak, such as widows, divorced wives, and orphans. Legal penalties were based on retribution ('an eye for an eye and a tooth for a tooth'). If a house fell down, killing the owner, the builder was executed; if its fall killed the owner's son, the builder's son was executed. The system placed revenge for injuries in the hands of the government, to prevent private blood feuds.

Early orthodontics
Ancient Egyptians suffered from badly worn amd severely decayed teeth, caused by chewing hard plant material and by sand in their food. Egyptian texts refer to the use of wire to hold teeth in place and prevent them from falling out.

Misplaced camels

Abraham's people were neither true nomads, like modern Bedouin who roam the desert with their camels, nor settled farmers, but semi-nomads, moving seasonally between the desert and the cooler hills. Genesis says they used camels, but these were probably not domesticated in the Middle East until c.1000 B.C., well after the time of the Exodus. Instead, they had donkeys, unsuitable for long desert journeys, but able to cover some 20mi (32km) a day. Genesis's mention of camels is one of many clues that the book was written long after the events it describes.

Decoding hieroglyphics

When Christianity reached Egypt, use of the hieroglyphic script began to fade. By A.D. 300 no one could read it, and this remained true until 1822. In 1799 a French soldier, digging a fort on the Nile, uncovered the Rosetta Stone – a basalt stele inscribed in hieroglyphs, in a simplified Egyptian script (demotic), and in Greek. Scholars found that all three were translations of the same text: after years of study, French Egyptologist Jean Francois Champollion (1790-1832) 'cracked the code.'

Breaking eggs

Old Kingdom Egyptians revered the white ibis as sacred. The birds were kept in temples and mummified when they died – more than 4 million ibis mummies were found at Hermopolis alone. In the Middle Kingdom, a new priesthood set out to destroy the ibis cult. Killing an ibis carried the death penalty, but by claiming that ibis eggs hatched basilisks

(fabulous monsters whose glance killed) the priests were able to order wholesale destruction of eggs and nests. Thus the sacred ibis was exterminated in Egypt.

War horses

Egypt lacked any tradition of horse-breeding on a large scale, but when the Hyksos kings introduced war chariots, very many horses were needed. An obvious source of both chariots and livestock was the enemy lines. After the Battle of Megiddo (1458 B.C.) it is recorded that the Egyptians took more than 2,200 horses from the defeated Canaanites as booty.

Babies in the bullrushes ▶

Babylonian clay tablets relate that the mother of Akkadian ruler Sargon the Great bore him in secret and laid him in a basket of rushes, waterproofed with bitumen, which she cast into the river. The Bible tells how the infant Moses (born probably some 1,000 years after Sargon's time) was born in secrecy, laid in a rush basket (made watertight with clay and tar), and left beside the Nile (right). Scholars believe the Hebrews adopted the story for Moses from legends of Sargon.

◀ Writers' workshops

When Sumer was absorbed into the Akkadian empire, Akkadian became the common language, but the Sumerian tongue was preserved for formal use (left). Writing schools, 'Houses of Tablets,' were set up to record Sumerian literature. Here a trained scholar, the 'father,' taught the basic skills of writing and grammar to new pupils, 'younger brothers,' and more advanced techniques to 'older brothers.'

Death feast

Grave goods in Egyptian tombs supplied everything the dead might need in the Afterlife – even food. A noblewoman's tomb at Saqqara, predating the Old Kingdom, contained a splendid feast, including bread, barley porridge, stewed fruit, beef, fish, quail, a dish of kidneys, pigeon stew, and honey cakes.

Potent medicine

From around the time of the Crusades (11th century A.D. onward) the mummified remains of ancient Egyptians were in increasing demand in western Europe – but not for their archeological interest. 'Mummy,' made from their powdered bones, was valued as a wonder working medicine, and in particular as a potent sex stimulant.

Pet cemetery

The Egyptian practice of mummification was not reserved for humans: sacred birds and animals, from crocodiles to cats, received the treatment on a vast scale. 19th-century archeologists found so many mummified cats that they lost interest. Some 300,000 feline mummies from a cat cemetery at Beni Hassan were ground up for fertilizer: only one specimen survives.

SUPERFACTS

Gender confusion

Egypt had one woman pharaoh, Hatshepsut (c.1473-58 BC). With no precedent for a female ruler, she became an honorary man. She wore male dress, was portrayed with a beard, and, because the word 'pharaoh' was grammatically masculine, wrote, and presumably spoke, of herself as male.

Air conditioned tombs

many of the monuments of ancient Egypt, after enduring for centuries, are endangered today. Some, preserved for centuries under the sand, are crumbling because of airborne or underground moisture – like the world-famous Sphinx at Giza. Tombs sealed for centuries have suffered from the entry of air, and moisture from tourists' breath. Open-air monuments could be protected by trenches and pumps to prevent water seepage, or by bonding the stones with silicon compounds; although some say the only way to save the Sphinx may be to bury it again. Experts urge stricter controls on visitors to tombs, and air conditioning to control temperature and humidity.

Pets of pedigree

The cat (right), perhaps the most universal pet of the modern world, was first domesticated by the Egyptians. One modern breed, the spotted Egyptian Mau, is said to be directly descended from the cats of Ancient Egypt. The Egyptians were perhaps the first people to produce distinct breeds of domestic livestock. Among their bequests in this line to the modern world is the greyhound.

Egypt's Book of Proverbs

An Egyptian text, 'The Wisdom of Amenemope' – written down in c.750 B.C., but based on a much earlier work – records a wise man's advice to his son. Resemblances between its words of wisdom and those of the Bible's Book of Proverbs suggest it influenced the latter.

The march of iron

The end of the Hittite Empire (c.1200 B.C.) brought the gift of iron to other nations. The Hittites had reserved the secret of iron-working for centuries; now smiths and their craft spread across the Middle East, transforming both warfare and agriculture, with iron swords and plowshares.

Slanderous story

Greek geographer Herodotus (c.484-425 B.C.) visited the Great Pyramid of Cheops some 2,000 years after it was built, and saw it as a memorial to tyranny. In his account, Cheops was a wicked ruler who, needing money, forced his daughter into prostitution. While earning money for him, she also demanded from each client one stone towards her own memorial — one of the three lesser pyramids beside the Great Pyramid (below). In fact, these monuments were raised for Cheops's wives.

Slums in Canaan

Early Israelite cities in Canaan were the work of amateur builders new to urban life. They did not know how to build soundly, lay out streets, or instal drains. Their houses were small, dark, and airless, with mud walls and brushwood roofs. Narrow alleys between, without drainage or paving, were awash with mud; household garbage raised the street level above the ground floor of many houses.

Sexism defied

Israelite laws regarded women as mere property, like other livestock. A woman was owned first by her father (who could sell her into slavery), then by her husband (who could divorce her without explanation or maintenance). But the Old Testament makes it clear that, in practice, strong-minded women like Sarah, Miriam, Deborah, Jael, Huldah, and others were held in respect and acted in many ways as men's equals.

Routed by rats

Sennacherib suffered again from divine intervention. Egyptian legend tells how the the creator god Ptah prevented him from capturing the city of Pelusium. Ptah sent an army of rats to gnaw through the Assyrians' bowstrings and shield handles: weaponless, they had to retreat.

The 'Black Obelisk'

The campaigns of Assyrian king Shalmaneser III (859-825 B.C.) were recorded on stone. A stele known as the 'Black Obelisk' depicts King Jehu of Israel paying homage – the first known picture of a Semite in traditional costume.

Judgment on Jordan

The mound of Tel Dan marks the remains of the Canaanite city of Laish, founded some 5,000 years ago and renamed by the Israelite tribe of Dan when they captured it. Its Arab name, Tel el-Kadi, 'Hill of the Judge,' comes from a legend telling how God sat there to settle an argument between the Dan, Banias, and Hatzbani Rivers over which was greatest. They accepted his judgement – 'Unite, and you will surely become the most important river' – joining to form the Jordan River.

Solomon's stables

Excavations at Megiddo uncovered well-planned stables of the 9th century B.C., which housed some 450 animals in four blocks. Each block is divided into units, where the horses stood in spacious cobbled stalls with limestone mangers, facing each other across a central paved passage. Tradition ascribes these stables to Solomon, but research suggests that some at least were more probably built for the later King Ahab.

One thousand gods ▶

The Hittites recognized not only their own deities (right), like the Storm God and Sun Goddess, but the gods of practically every people with whom they came into contact. This produced a vast pantheon of divinities: indeed, the Hittite peace treaty with Egypt invoked 'one thousand gods' as witnesses.

A race of giants

Goliath, the Philistine champion slain by young David, was 'six cubits and a span' in height. With a variable cubit measure, this makes him between 9.75ft (2.97m) and 11.25ft (3.43m) tall. Genesis records that 'there were giants in the earth' before the Flood. According to Hebrew legend, King Og of Bashan, of a giant tribe called the Rephaim, was so tall that he walked beside Noah's Ark through the Flood.

Illustrious ancestors

Emperor Haile Selassie of Ethiopia (1892-1975) claimed descent from the Old Testament's Queen of Sheba, who visited King Solomon. He was outdone by a medieval French nobleman who claimed kinship with the Virgin Mary. He commissioned a painting, still in existence, showing himself with the Virgin. A comic-strip type 'balloon' from her mouth says: '*Bonjour, mon cousin*' (Good day, cousin').

Elephants at war

War elephants were used by both the Ptolemies and the Seleucids. They carried small towers with archers into battle, but more important was their intimidating presence. The Seleucids used Indian elephants whose mahouts had generations of experience; the Ptolemies' African elephants were smaller and less docile. The Seleucids' elephants probably helped them defeat Judas Maccabeus at Beth-Zachariah in 162 B.C. This was their last use in war – but they continued to feature on Seleucid coinage as emblems of power.

The moving temple ▼

Ramses II's rock temple at Abu Simbel (below) was one of the greatest works of the New Kingdom. Cut out of a cliff, it extended 200ft (61m) into the rock. Four colossal statues of Ramses guarded its towering entrance, and its walls bore reliefs of Rameses' victories – including some 1,500 carved and painted soldiers. In the 1960s, when the Aswan Dam drowned the area, it became necessary to rescue the temple (and 22 others). It was moved and rebuilt in exactly the same orientation – so that twice a year the rising sun illuminates statues seated in the inner sanctuary.

SUPERFACTS

Battle lords ▼

Mounted infantry (riding to battle on horseback or in large carts, but usually dismounting to fight) were the core of Assyria's army. Maintaining a supply of remounts was so vital that 100 horses per day were requisitioned from all over the empire. Most of Assyria's battles ended when the defenders took refuge in a stronghold – and few forts could withstand Assyrian siege towers (below), hand-propelled 'tanks,' and missile-throwing engines. When Hezekiah of Judah was besieged in Jerusalem by the Assyrian King Sennacherib, the city was saved only when the besieging army was struck by plague – brought by 'the Angel of the Lord to save His people.'

Royal huntsmen ▶

Assyrian king Tiglath-pileser recorded that he killed 120 lions on foot and 800 more from his war chariot (right). From earliest times, such royal hunts symbolized, through the slaughter of fierce beasts, the king's power to slay human foes.

Sabbath slaughter

In the early days of the Maccabite rebellion, one group of Jews hid from the Seleucid armies in the desert. Tracked down on the Sabbath day, they did not defend themselves – for Jewish law forbids all work (which they took to include fighting) on the Sabbath. More than 1,000 were killed, preferring death to betrayal of their faith.

False witness

Many early Christians were martyred for their faith, but others (*lapsi*; 'lapsed ones') escaped death by agreeing to sacrifice to Roman gods. Those who actually did so were called *thurificati* ('incense-bearers'). *Libellatici* ('holders of certificates') avoided the act, but bribed officials to get certificates of sacrifice.

The golden temple

Herod the Great's Temple at Jerusalem was meant to impress the Roman world with his wealth and power, as well as to please his Jewish subjects. Built to the same plan as Solomon's Temple, it stood twice as high, and Herod extended the platform on which it stood to cover some 35 acres (14ha) – perhaps the largest religious enclosure of the ancient world. The Temple itself was of white marble, covered with gold inside and out: even the spikes on the roof, to discourage birds, were of gold. The building program began in 19 B.C., and was not completed until c.A.D. 62. Eight years later it was looted and destroyed by the Romans.

St. Pontius Pilate

Although he is infamous for having condemned Jesus to death, suprisingly little is known of Pontius Pilate, Roman governor of Judaea in A.D. 26-36. Several legends tell of his remorseful suicide; but another says that he died penitent. The latter version is preferred by the Coptic (Eyptian Christian) Church, which regards him as a holy martyr. The Greek Orthodox Church reveres Pilate's wife, Procla, who is said to have become a Christian, as a saint.

Blessed beasts

The ox and donkey that attended the Nativity entered Christian symbolism. The ox stood for sacrifice. The donkey was a valued mount in the East, where it often represented peace; in the donkey-despising West it was seen as a symbol of humility.

'King Cole's' daughter? ▶

Helena (far right) (c.255-330), mother of Emperor Constantine the Great, may have influenced her son's championship of Christianity. Legend says she was British, daughter of King Coel of Colchester (sometimes identified as the merry-making 'Old King Cole' of nursery rhyme) – though this is unlikely. Now revered as St. Helen, she is traditionally credited with the discovery of the True Cross on which Jesus died, and the Holy Sepulcher, at Jerusalem in 326.

Down with sport!

The spread of Greco-Roman culture brought public entertainment to Palestine. Herod gave Jerusalem a stadium for gladiatorial sports and an amphitheater for chariot races. Most Jews disapproved the introduction of athletics because of pagan associations and the offensive (to them) nudity of competitors.

Prayer of two creeds

Christianity and Judaism were long seen as opposing faiths. Yet Jesus's teachings derive closely from Judaic beliefs of His time. His pacifism and rejection of worldly wealth accord with the beliefs of the Essenes (pages 64-65). The Lord's Prayer, supreme prayer of Christianity, echoes the words of Rabbi Philo of Alexandria (c.20 B.C.-c.A.D. 54), who wrote: 'If you ask pardon for your sins, you must also forgive those who sin against you.'

Waiting for Messiah

Orthodox Jews see Jesus as a great but mortal teacher, and believe Messiah is yet to come. In 1643, a wealthy Jew, Baruch Mizrachi, instructed his heirs to

preserve his Jerusalem house forever, so it would be ready for him when Messiah's coming called him from his grave. It was destroyed in Israel's 1948 War of Independence, but in 1977, Mizrachi's descendants were allowed to replace it with a small wooden house in the Jewish Quarter to ensure that his wishes were met.

Bloodless victory

In c.429 British churchmen alarmed by the spread of the Pelagian heresy called St. Germanus, Bishop of Auxerre, from France to combat it. According to legend, Germanus led a weaponless band of British Christians against a host of heretical, armed Picts and Saxons. On seeing the enemy, Germanus's rabble raised such a loud shout of praise that their opponents fled in terror. The bloodless triumph was called the 'Hallelujah Victory.' Unhappily, the Church authorities' intolerance of any belief they considered heretical led to many more savage battles.

Symbols of Jewry

Although the *Magen David* ('Star of David') is believed to be ancient, it is mentioned neither in the Bible nor the Talmud. It did not become the universal symbol of Jewry until modern times. Previously the *Menorah* (seven-branched candlestick) or Tables of the Ten Commandments were taken by the Jews as symbols of identity.

Apostles' tombs

Rome claims the graves of six of the twelve original Apostles: Bartholomew, James the Less, Jude, Peter, Philip, and Simon – plus Matthias (successor to Judas) and Paul. The graves of Andrew, Matthew, and Thomas are claimed by Naples; that of Luke by Padua; and Mark's supposed remains were buried at Venice in c.800. Italy lacks only Judas (presumably in an unmarked grave in Jerusalem), and James the Great, whose tomb is at Compostella, Spain, where he is revered as Santiago.

◀ Holy errors

In early and medieval times, churches and wealthy individuals erected special buildings and made jeweled boxes (reliquaries) (left) to house holy relics, most often the bones of saints. Some must have been genuine, but fakes abounded. Among the most in demand were fragments of the True Cross: enough existed to add up to a forest. Unscrupulous salesmen offered feathers from Archangel Gabriel's wings; flasks of the Virgin Mary's milk; even twigs from the 'burning bush' out of which God spoke to Moses.

INDEX

Page numbers in **bold** indicate major references including accompanying photographs. Page numbers in *italics* indicate captions to illustrations. Other entries are in normal type.

A 17th century painting portrays the Holy Trinity: Father, Son, and Holy Ghost. Several early Christian heresies arose from difficulties with this complex doctrine.

PICTURE CREDITS

The publishers wish to thank the following agencies who have supplied
photographs for this book. The photographs have been credited by page
number and, where necessary, by position on the page: B(Bottom),
T(Top), L(Left), BR(Bottom Right), etc.

Ancient Art & Architecture Collection: 10, 12-13, 14-15, 16, 16-17, 17(BR), 18-19(B), 19, 20(T), 21(B), 22-3(T), 22-3(B), 26, 27(BR), 28, 30, 30-31, 31(T), 32(T), 34-5, 35(B), 35(R), 36, 36-7, 37, 38(T), 40, 40-41, 41, 42(L), 46, 46-7, 47(L), 49(B), 50, 51(L), 55, 56, 56-7(T), 56-7(B), 57(TL), 58, 59(B), 61(L), 62, 64, 64-5, 65(R), 67(BL), 69(B), 69(T), 72-3(B), 73(B), 74, 75, 80(T), 82, 83(TL), 83(TR), 84, 85(TL), 86, 86-7(B), 88, 89, 90-91(B), 92, 93(T), 96-7, 97(B), 103, 105

Art Resource: 2-3, 5, 6, 7, 11(B), 14, 15, 18, 18-19(T), 22, 24, 24-5, 25, 27(L), 27(TR), 28-29, 29, 31(B), 32-3, 35(T), 33, 38(B),
38-39, 39, 43(L), 43(R), 50-51, 52-3(B), 54, 59(T), 67(T), 71(TL), 71(TR), 78(L), 80(B), 81, 83(C), 83(B), 85(B), 85(TR), 88-9, 92-3, 96, 97(T), 99(TL), 99(B), 100, 101, 102(T), 104(T), 107, 110-111

The Bettmann Archive: 76(B), 94, 95(B)

FPG International: 23, 53(T), 72-3(T)

The Granger Collection: 86-7(T), 87(T), 91

Israel Museum, Jerusalem: 78(R), 78-79, 79(BL)

NASA: 17(BL)

North Wind Picture Archives: 51(R), 72, 73(T)

Photo Researchers, Inc.: 11(T), 12, 54-5, 60, 63, 65(L), 66(T), 67(BR), 68-9, 71(B), 74-5, 79(R), 90, 90-91(T), 98, 99(TR), 102(B)

Seth Joel: 13(R)

Zev Radovan: 8, 13(L), 20(B), 21(T), 42(R), 42-3, 44, 44-5, 45, 47(R), 48, 49(T), 53(B), 57(TR), 61(R), 62-3, 66(L), 68, 70, 70-71, 76(T), 77, 95(B), 104(B)

Map artwork on pages 21, 27, 29, 40, 47, 51, 52, 55, 57, 63, 75 by Peter Bull.